CW00395211

The
Romney Files

BRETT ARENDS

Copyright © 2012 Brett Arends

Cover photograph © iStockPhoto/EdStock/Chip Somodevilla

All rights reserved.

ISBN: 1479100919
ISBN-13: 978-1479100910

DEDICATION

To the folks Ted Williams called "the knights of the keyboard" – Boston's newsmen and women, past and present.

CONTENTS

ACKNOWLEDGMENTS

This book wouldn't have been possible without my wife, who was both an amazing support, as ever, and a terrific editor. Many others also played a valuable part. My thanks to my former Boston Herald colleagues Jennifer Powell, Eric Convey, and Cosmo Macero, who offered excellent suggestions, and were a great help with the editing. Yes, we got the band back together. Thanks, too, to my friend Matt Black for help with the cover. In a broader sense I owe a debt to all my former colleagues at the Herald, and to our rivals across town at the Boston Globe, who covered Romney's career so well for so long. I owe a particular debt to the Globe's Michael Kranish and Scott Helman, whose biography, *The Real Romney*, explained a lot about Mitt Romney's first presidential campaign that had puzzled the rest of us.

i

1

INTRODUCTION

In 2006, as Mitt Romney was contemplating his first run for the White House, I sat down for breakfast with one of the senior figures in the Massachusetts Republican party. He told me how Romney helped blow his 1994 Senate race against Ted Kennedy.

A few weeks before voting, Romney was trailing in the polls, but the race was still close. Everything hinged on the first televised debate, to take place in Faneuil Hall in downtown Boston. But when Romney and his advisers met to prepare, my breakfast companion said, the candidate seemed disturbingly nonchalant.

"I kept warning him that this was going to be a very substantive debate," my companion recalled. But Romney wouldn't take it in. The 47-year-old chief executive of Bain Capital seemed to think he'd be just fine, and that he could pretty much wing it.

Kennedy cleaned his clock. During the debate the veteran senator was confident, polished, and the master of his subject. Romney, meanwhile, looked amateurish, out of step, and bewildered. The race was over that night. In mid-September Romney and Kennedy had been neck and neck in the polls. In early November, he lost to Kennedy by 17 points – in a year which saw Republican landslides around the country.

Romney later admitted: "I was getting ready for this guy that was going to be kind of a doddering old fool. I'd be able to crush him like a grape." Instead Kennedy crushed him.

Fast forward eighteen years, to the summer of 2012. As I am putting the finishing touches to this manuscript, Mitt Romney is being pummeled by the Democrats over his tax returns and mysterious finances. How much tax has he paid in the past? How much money did he have offshore? What maneuvers did he use to build up an IRA worth tens of millions of dollars?

President Barack Obama should logically be trailing in the polls. The economy is in the trough. Recent jobs figures have been terrible. Yet instead the president is leading – in large part due to the continued missteps, and astonishingly poor preparation, by Mitt Romney.

The Republican nominee has been running for president for at least six years – and, informally, for much longer than that. He claims a long career as an experienced, hands-on executive. Yet he still looks like he's trying to wing it. Why didn't he put his finances in order years ago? Why hasn't he prepared for the race?

I've been following Mitt Romney for nearly twenty years, since the Kennedy campaign. My family has lived in New England for decades. I was a reporter and columnist for the Boston Herald while Romney was governor of Massachusetts. (While there I upset the administration by reporting that the states, on Romney's watch, had the 47th worst record of jobs creation in the country.) Since 2007 I've written about finance – including Romney's private equity and hedge fund worlds – for the Wall Street Journal, and for its sister publications MarketWatch and Smart Money. I have a background in Romney's industry, as well. Romney began his career as a strategy consultant at Bain & Co. I used to work for their bigger competitor, McKinsey & Co.

Who is Mitt Romney? What does he really stand for? What kind of president would he actually be? This book offers a view.

To most Americans, his real record and career is largely unknown. And yet here he is, locked in a tight race for the White House. David Paleologos at Suffolk University, one of the best pollsters in the country, argues that the race could go down to the wire. The polls are tight in the critical battleground states, like Ohio and Florida.

So much of Mitt Romney's past is a closed book. He spent much of his career in private business, out of the public eye. He frequently calls himself a "businessman," an "executive," a "venture capitalist," and a "private equity" man. He worked at Bain & Co., the strategy consultants, and Bain Capital, the private equity company. Both are secretive private partnerships. They rarely talk to strangers or the media. Their records are not open to scrutiny. The political media rarely delve that deeply either. These companies are a long way from their beat.

The Romney team aggressively controls media access and inquiry. In his book *Turnaround*, Romney wrote that when he was in charge of the Salt Lake City Olympics he was very open to the media and held a press conference every week. If that was true, those days are long gone. The candidate doesn't open up to questions, and his entourage, led by his press secretary Eric Fehrnstrom, keeps the media at bay. Anyone who doubts that should see the 2007 YouTube footage where Glen Johnson, then a reporter at the Associated Press, tried to press Romney on an issue. Fehrnstrom, and even Romney, turned aggressive. Romney went up to Johnson afterward to argue with him. Fehrnstrom told the reporter to act more professionally.

Ronald Scott, a former Time magazine reporter, wrote a biography, *Mitt Romney: An Inside Look At The Man And his Politics*, in 2011. Scott knows Romney. They are fellow Mormons in the Boston area. Yet Scott called his book "one of the toughest reporting assignments of my life." The Romney campaign stonewalled him. He got no access to the candidate. They even ignored fact-checking emails. He was cut out.

As for Bain Capital: The media has reported on the occasional company it bought – usually because it had layoffs, such as Ampad, or folded, like GS Steel. The Romney campaign has responded by pointing to more positive stories, such as Staples, the office supply chain, which Bain Capital helped finance in the early days. Mitt Romney has claimed that "net, net" the businesses in which Bain Capital invested while he was running it have created "over 100,000 jobs," but it is a claim that has no backup. "Restore Our Future," the pro-Romney Super Political Action Committee (PAC), ran commercials in Iowa claiming Romney "helped create thousands of jobs" when he was at Bain Capital. When Factcheck.org, the website which tries to hold public figures accountable, asked the Super PAC for the facts to back up the assertion, a spokeswoman replied: "We aren't supplying that information."

Early in 2012, Eric Fehrnstrom said that an election campaign was like an Etch-A-Sketch®: Once the primaries were over and the general election race began, he said, everything got shaken up and you started again with a blank slate.

This is not in the interests of voters. Even as we watch the campaign over the coming months, we should take a look at what went before. What did the candidate say and do in the past? How did he get here?

I've delved into my notebooks and recollections from my time at the Herald, and into my work since, to try to find some answers.

As early as 2004 I assumed that Romney was angling to run for president. It is forgotten now, but in the early days he was seen by the national media as a hopeless long-shot. I never thought so. I saw all the advantages he could bring to a national race, against a very weak 2008 field.

You see a little more when you cover a politician locally. Apart from anything else, you get to see him when the national media isn't around.

Most people know Romney as a man whose campaign appearances are so awkward that even his supporters cringe with embarrassment. Yet I saw him turn up to the St. Patrick's Day breakfast in South Boston in March, 2006, a Mormon Republican in a room full of Irish Catholic Democrats, and bring down the house.

I remember following Romney up to New Hampshire, on a bitterly cold New England Sunday in the fall of 2006. The mid-term elections were a few days away. The Republican party was headed for a massive defeat across the country. But I got in my car and schlepped up north to a small church hall, on a dark road, way out of in the middle of nowhere, just to watch Mitt Romney campaign for a handful of small-time politicians who were guaranteed to lose anyway.

The whole thing had the air of a wake. About two hundred gloomy activists were crammed into a small room with a low ceiling. Charlie Bass, the sitting Republican congressman, gave what was effectively a concession speech – two days before the election. While he talked I scanned a campaign leaflet one of his volunteers had given me at the door. Bass, it said, was an "independent voice for New Hampshire." Nowhere on the pamphlet did it mention that he was a Republican. That's one way you know a party is in trouble. Next up was a local politician running for governor. He gave a brave, peppy speech, but nobody was fooled. He was days away from losing in a 2-1 landslide.

As the speeches dragged on, my eyes wandered over to Mitt and Ann Romney, standing in the middle of the crowd. At the time, Romney was the chairman of the Republican Governors' Association. It gave him a high national profile within the party. The couple had spent weeks crisscrossing the country, campaigning for doomed Republican candidates. It must have been exhausting. Ann, of course, has multiple sclerosis, but she stood by Mitt's side, smiling. They stood there for over an hour so that Mitt could make a pointless five minute speech for a lost cause, and shake the hands of a lot of strangers in New Hampshire. As I watched, Mitt quietly reached over and gave Ann's shoulder a squeeze.

The event got me thinking. I knew why I had made the trip: I was watching Romney as he laid the groundwork to run for president. But why was Romney there? We still don't know. It can hardly be ideological passion that drives him. Rarely has a politician been so flexible. Nor can it be a burning desire for power. He was the chief executive of Massachusetts for four years, but apparently grew bored of the job within a few months. Is it a desire to be famous, or to avenge his father's famous political defeat in 1968? Pure ego? Amateur psychologists can take their guesses.

Politics these days takes an impossible toll on any serious candidate – rich or poor, Republican or Democrat. Anyone running for president must throw away years of their lives on grueling, thankless trips like this: Meeting after meeting, speech after speech. Even if you are so rich you have a private plane, it's still a terrible grind. The chances you'll succeed are slim. In 2006 the Romneys were in their late fifties and very rich. They could have been relaxing on a yacht in the Florida Keys, enjoying the sunset. Romney could have been in Silicon Valley, financing interesting new startups. He could have been raising money for a valuable nonprofit, helping transform lives. Instead the couple were standing in this cramped little room in the New England cold, eating mouthfuls of mediocre lasagna, listening to a boring speech by a man who would never be the governor of New Hampshire.

This book takes a critical look at Romney's record in public life. But it also takes a close look at his much longer career in business, and includes information you haven't read anywhere else. The findings challenge a lot of the conventional wisdom about Mitt Romney.

Four years ago the American public went to the polls and elected a president they barely knew. Barack Obama, when he won in 2008, was an enigma to most voters. He had been a senator for just four years, and had spent nearly half that time campaigning. And the media didn't vet him too closely. Obama had a thin resume, but it didn't get scrutinized. Many voters just projected on to him their own hopes instead. Since the election they've learned more about him. Some of them – some moderates, and some liberals – have been disappointed.

It's time to take a serious look at Mitt Romney's resume.

This book, while highly critical of Mitt Romney, is not written from a liberal perspective or a conservative one. I do not, for example, criticize Bain Capital for laying people off, or criticize Romney for saying he is pro-life on abortion, or object in any way to him being rich. Instead I try to hold him up to his own standards. I measure his performance in business by the yardsticks he would apply to others. You are not asked to take anything on faith. I subject Romney's record to the "fact-based analysis" used at Bain. I look at his record on religion, not by the standards of an evangelical Christian or a secular liberal, but by the standards he himself applies. I look at his record in Massachusetts not from the point of view of the Democratic or Republican parties, but from the point of view of New Englanders who lived through it – the good and the bad.

Maybe what America needs right now is a smart, tough, pragmatic CEO in the White House. Our tax code is broken. We're not creating jobs like we used to. The federal government has become a sprawling mess. And unless we take action now, everyone agrees Social Security and Medicare are going to run into trouble very fast.

But if the country could do with a CEO, is Mitt Romney the one we need?

This book is tough. I hope it will provoke thought and debate among friends and critics alike. But be aware it takes sides. Why haven't I written a book like this about Obama? The short answer is that I have nothing to say about Obama that isn't already known. If, after reading this, you end up cynical about both of the main candidates for president, don't blame me.

2

WHAT'S THE MATTER WITH NEW HAMPSHIRE?

Drive north out of Boston over the Leonard P. Zakim bridge. On your left you'll pass the Boston Garden sports arena, home of the Celtics and the Bruins. Off to your right you can see the U.S. Constitution and the old Charlestown naval yard. Rising up to meet you is Bunker Hill, topped by the great stone monument.

Keep going north on this road and you'll be in New Hampshire within half an hour.

If you don't know New England, or you don't spend much time here, it's easy to forget that the states are very small. They are all crowded together cheek-by-jowl in an area smaller than Kansas. The southeastern third of New Hampshire, where most of the state's population lives, is an extended Boston suburb. Thousands of commuters take Route 93 north every evening, as they head home over the border.

Mitt Romney has taken this road many times, both as a

governor and as a private citizen. He's had a weekend home in New Hampshire since the mid-1990s. He spent time there before that. He's been campaigning there for at least the last six years. It's almost his home state.

Most of this seemed to be overlooked in January, 2012. For the week leading up to the New Hampshire primary, the national media flocked into the state from New York, Washington and points beyond, crowding into a few blocks in downtown Manchester. On primary night, after Romney had racked up 39% of the vote, the commentators thought it was a huge win.

"He ran the table," said a breathless political analyst on CNN that night. "He won with Republicans, with people who identify themselves as conservatives, Tea Party supporters, evangelicals, and of course, those very important independent voters."

MSNBC's Chris Matthews called the win, following a narrow victory in Iowa, an "historic feat."

"Mitt Romney won big in the New Hampshire primary," said Fox's Bill O'Reilly. He "now appears to be unstoppable," he added. Comedian Dennis Miller, appearing with O'Reilly, called Romney's 39% of the vote "a super nice score."

But was it?

This is Romney's back yard. I used to live in New Hampshire. The home major league baseball team is the Boston Red Sox. The hockey team is the Bruins. The football team is the Patriots. The network news comes from Boston too. When Romney was governor of Massachusetts, he spent more time on the air in New Hampshire than did the state's own governor, John Lynch.

Yet, against one of the weakest fields of candidates ever assembled by a major political party, Romney couldn't even rack up two-fifths of the vote in the state's Republican primary.

He's been working New Hampshire for years. He's been

handing out campaign checks for local Republican candidates, turning out for fund-raisers, helping out where he can. As I saw during the 2006 midterm elections, when Republicans were heading to certain defeat across the country, he was still up there in cold October nights stumping for doomed candidates, earning favors.

The people of New Hampshire know Romney better than the voters in Massachusetts do. He's been schmoozing them hard since at least 2004. He spent $3 million trying to win them over in the 2008 primary, and another $1.2 million – says the Associated Press – campaigning there in 2012.

In the end, in 2012, he was able to secure just 97,500 votes. That's about $43 per vote.

Forget the conventional wisdom on national TV from New York, or the opinions of the pundits in Washington, D.C. If Mitt Romney was such a successful governor in Massachusetts, how come even the Republican voters on his doorstep don't want to vote for him?

Romney's Pitch

In the 2012 elections, Mitt Romney's core message is pretty simple. He's a successful business guy with 25 years' real-world experience in the economy. He knows how to get the economy moving again, and to bring back jobs. His opponent, on the other hand, is a career politician who's never had a real job.

"[I'm] someone who's been a leader in the private sector and knows how the economy works at the grassroots level," he said in a debate in South Carolina in January, 2012. His rivals – then Gingrich, now Obama – were, he said, men who have "spent their life in Washington."

Or, as he put it in a debate in September, 2011, "I spent my life in business. I know how jobs come, how jobs go."

Speaking in Michigan in May, 2012, he promised to reinvigorate America "as an economic powerhouse." His "pro-growth" policies on taxes, regulations and labor, he said, would produce "a revival in American manufacturing" and a dynamic, fast growth economy. "So-called gazelle, or fast-growing, businesses will spring up across the country," he said, offering "new jobs....higher wages and better benefits."

It sounds very appealing. It's just what the country needs. To the people in New England, however, it is also very, very familiar.

Ten years ago, Massachusetts – like America today – was struggling. The collapse of the high-tech boom had hit it hard. From the summer of 2000 through the summer of 2002, the state lost tens of thousands of jobs. The unemployment rate doubled. The fallout was felt throughout the region.

An ailing state turned its hopeful eyes to the white knight in shining armor riding in on his horse from Salt Lake City.

"I am urging, pleading, no, outright begging," wrote Brian McGrory, the influential columnist for the Boston Globe, in February, 2002. "When the Olympic flame in Salt Lake finally dies, when the athletes are done and gone, when the proceeds are totaled into a surplus, please, Mitt Romney, get on the next plane out of town. Come back to Massachusetts and run for governor."

McGrory was hardly alone. Many prominent figures in the Bay State urged Romney to join the race. He seemed to be everything the state needed: A clean outsider, untainted by Beacon Hill, a businessman with real can-do experience and expertise.

Romney seized his chance, coming back to Boston and entering the race for governor. Securing the Republican nomination was no problem at all. In the general election he found himself in a battle against Democrat Shannon

O'Brien, the state treasurer.

Romney's pitch was that he alone, thanks to his business experience, could bring back jobs and growth.

"I've spent my life in the economy," he told Boston business leaders in a meeting downtown, the Globe reported in October, 2002. "I'm someone who knows how the economy grows, why companies decide to move somewhere, why they decide to leave somewhere...I speak the language of business."

Ever the consultant, he even set up an overhead projector in the Omni Parker House hotel – a landmark Victorian hotel down the road from the State House, and one of JFK's old haunts – to show them how he planned to turn around the state's economy. In a PowerPoint presentation he promised to create a "circle of prosperity."

In a refrain that would later become very familiar, he contrasted his record as a "jobs creator" in the "real economy" of the private sector with the record of O'Brien, a "career politician," an "insider."

Romney promised in his campaign to be a tireless salesman for the state, traveling everywhere – "inside Massachusetts, outside Massachusetts, outside of our country, to encourage businesses to come grow and thrive in the most robust portion of the economy – Massachusetts!"

As he contrasted himself with his "career politician" rival, he piled it on. "I don't have to wait in the lobby to see middle management," he said, in his most pointed comment. "There's virtually not a chief executive officer in the country that won't let me in to sit down with them, in their office, to pitch Massachusetts."

The image of Shannon O'Brien sitting in the lobby waiting to meet middle management, while Mitt Romney was being ushered into the CEO's office as an old friend, was indelible.

"My program for creating jobs," Romney promised

voters, *"is second to none in the entire history of this state."*(Italics added.)

Who wouldn't be tempted by such an offer?

Romney took his message to the airwaves. "We need every kind of good-paying job," Romney told the voters in one TV commercial. "As governor, I'll reduce taxes and change our job-growth strategy, so we can attract good jobs from big companies, small companies, all companies."

Romney hadn't yet settled on the "from day one" pitch he would later use in his campaign for president, but even in 2002 he was getting there. He promised to spend the "first 60 days" of his administration on an aggressive campaign to sell the state as a business destination to corporate executives around the country, trying to persuade them to expand in Massachusetts.

It was the first try-out of the pitch he would take national ten years later.

For many Massachusetts voters, Romney's words sounded like welcome news. It was a tight election, but in the end Romney beat O'Brien by five points. Massachusetts voters chose the CEO who knew how to create jobs.

What did they get?

You can measure success and failure in any number of ways. Politicians – of both parties – are fond of measuring their opponents against giants and themselves against pygmies.

By some measures Massachusetts performed OK during the Romney years. High school students, as Romney likes to point out, did well in national tests. The state became the first in the union to achieve near-universal health insurance.

But how did the economy do? How far did Romney, the "real world businessman," deliver on his promises to bring back growth and jobs?

According to the U.S. Department of Labor, while Mitt Romney was governor of Massachusetts the state ranked 47th out of all 50 states in America in terms of percentage jobs growth. The only states that did worse were Michigan, Ohio, and Katrina-hit Louisiana – in other words, two rustbelt states losing factory jobs to China, and one whose principal city was washed away by a flood.

When Mitt Romney took office in January, 2003, 3.23 million people in Massachusetts had jobs, according to the Labor Department. When Romney left office at the start of January, 2007, that number had risen by just 31,000 to 3.26 million.

This was total growth of just 1% over four years. Meanwhile New York State grew jobs by 2.8%, Georgia by 6.5%, Texas by 8.6%. Massachusetts ranked dead last among the states in New England. New Hampshire was up nearly 5%, Rhode Island 3%. Even sleepy Maine grew faster.

What is even more remarkable is that this gloomy picture actually flatters the true performance. That's because it includes an increase in the number of public sector workers in Massachusetts. That's hardly the boast a conservative private-sector businessman wants to make.

If you ignore those public sector jobs and look only at the "real world" private sector, Massachusetts ranked 48th out of 50. Only Michigan and Ohio did worse. Washington State, with a smaller population, created ten times as many private sector jobs.

Yes, even Louisiana did better – despite Hurricane Katrina. In September, 2005, New Orleans was effectively washed away. We all remember the scenes on TV – the chaos, the houses under water, the residents trying to escape. Louisiana had long been economically troubled, with the lowest bond rating in the country. This seemed like a death blow.

Yet despite this, the state had a better private sector jobs record from 2003 through 2006 than Massachusetts.

Meanwhile, according to the U.S. Commerce Department, the Massachusetts economy also ranked 47th in the country in terms of economic growth. From 2002 to 2006 the state's economy grew by less than 18%. Only Missouri, Ohio and Michigan did worse.

It was an astonishingly weak performance. Over the same period, the United States economy as a whole grew 50% faster than the Bay State.

Naturally, since he started running for president Mitt Romney has come under criticism for this. Texas governor Rick Perry, in his first debate in September, pointed out, "We created more jobs in the last three months in Texas than he created in four years in Massachusetts."

Perry added: "Michael Dukakis created jobs three times faster than you did, Mitt."

Romney has offered three defenses.

First, he has said he took over a terrible situation. "When I came in as governor, we were in a real freefall," he told the MSNBC debate in September, 2011. "We were losing jobs every month….We went to work as a team, and we were able to turn around the job losses. And at the end of four years, we had our unemployment rate down to 4.7 percent."

There is some truth to that. Massachusetts was certainly struggling when Romney took office. The state had been hit hard by the bursting of the dotcom bubble. However, the whole country had been hit by the recession. Most of it recovered. Was Massachusetts really hit harder by the collapse of the dotcom bubble than, say, California? From 2002 to 2006, California nonetheless grew jobs nearly five times as fast.

Romney's argument also contains an obvious weakness. His message on the campaign trail today is that he knows how to turn around a weak and struggling economy, such as the one we are in now. But the only time he has taken on that task before, he has not noticeably succeeded.

Romney's second defense has been to argue that at least the Massachusetts jobs number on his watch was positive, and that it compares favorably with the jobs lost so far under President Barack Obama. "At the end of four years," he told Republican voters in a debate in September, 2011, "we had our unemployment rate down to 4.7 percent. That's a record I think the president would like to see. As a matter of fact, we created more jobs in Massachusetts than this president has created in the entire country."

The performance of the U.S. job market on President Obama's watch has obviously been poor. Yet Mitt Romney's Massachusetts performed badly during a national – and global – economic boom, while the United States economy over the past four years has performed badly during a worldwide slump. You do not need to be partisan to see the difference.

From December, 2002 to December, 2006 America overall created 6.6 million jobs, an increase of 5%. The industries that did best nationwide included many where Massachusetts had big advantages – like higher education, financial services and biotechnology. So how come the Bay State missed out?

Romney's third line of defense has been to argue that many of the results of his "turnaround" took time to take effect, and that you couldn't see the benefits right away. He has said that some of the employers he had attracted to Massachusetts were "on their way" by the time he left office. However, if you stretch the performance period for, say, another year, the picture doesn't look any better. Measured from December, 2002 to December, 2007 Massachusetts still ranked 47th out of 50 in terms of total jobs growth. It was a bust.

Compared to the supertanker of the United States economy, Massachusetts is a light catamaran that should be easy to turn. The state is small, with high education and skill levels and some strong unique advantages. The difference between a boom and a slump is 50,000 jobs. Yet the state continued to hemorrhage jobs after Romney was elected.

The unemployment rate peaked in 2003, but not for good reasons. People were giving up and leaving the state. After the first two years of the Romney administration, we reported at the Boston Herald, Massachusetts had the distinction of being the only state in America that had actually lost population.

The state's jobs recession didn't really bottom out until the fall of 2004 – two years after Romney was elected. And the recovery that followed was anemic.

What happened? The Massachusetts economy had plenty of problems before Romney arrived, of course – like excessive zoning and regulations, strong unions, and lots of vested interests. At the Herald, I often interviewed local business owners struggling with crazy red tape. In his 2010 book *No Apology*, Mitt Romney recalls a businessman who had just expanded into Massachusetts telling him how bad the process had been.

These are important issues. But every state has its challenges. Mitt Romney certainly didn't cause these problems. He didn't do much to fix them either. The Bay State also came with a lot of advantages. Most states would give their eye-teeth to have local institutions like Harvard, the Massachusetts Institute of Technology, and Boston's hospitals. They're big employers, they're world leaders, and they're never going to get taken over, downsized, or relocated to China.

What is notable is that the Massachusetts economy fell short in those areas where you would have expected it to succeed under a governor who "talked the language of business" and boasted of a career as a "venture capitalist."

A conservative Boston think-tank, the Pioneer Institute, found that the real failure of the Romney economy in Massachusetts wasn't in the decline of the old economic dinosaurs. It was in the failure of the state to attract and encourage new and expanding businesses. "Massachusetts has developed an entrepreneurship problem," it reported in

"Failure To Thrive," an analysis of the state's economy up to 2007. That entrepreneurship problem, it said, plagued the state after 2002 – in other words, mostly while Mitt Romney was governor.

The new businesses, and their jobs, just dried up.

From the early 1990s to the early 2000s, the institute reported, new companies in Massachusetts had generated an average of about 200,000 new jobs a year. During the Romney years, the figure was less than 125,000. There was no recovery from the 2000-2 slump. In 2006-7, while the rest of the U.S. economy was growing at a healthy pace, Massachusetts entrepreneurs and small businesses were still in recession: They were creating fewer jobs than at any point since the crash of 1990-1. (Facebook, which was launched in a Harvard dorm around this time, quickly left for California.)

Governments don't create private sector jobs directly, but a lot of what they do affects whether risk-takers will create jobs. The Pioneer Institute concluded that the state government in these years had been doing the wrong things.

Romney had boasted on the campaign trail of all his contacts with big company CEOs. His friends in high places didn't help the state very much. From 2003 through 2006, companies relocated more jobs away from Massachusetts than the other way around, Pioneer calculated. Meanwhile, argued the institute, the Romney administration had spent too much time wooing big company bosses and not enough time encouraging and helping the small business owner.

"The focus for government efforts and incentives should be on...helping entrepreneurs to start business and helping existing companies to stay in business and expand," wrote the institute's John Friar and Megan Gay. "Firm relocation occupies too great a portion of the public sector's economic development attention...this attention is, at the very least, inefficiently directed and...a poor use of limited resources."

At the Herald, I interviewed the owner of a small business that New Hampshire governor John Lynch had snatched from Massachusetts, right under Romney's nose. The owner had been operating in Romney's own town of Belmont, Massachusetts, just down the road from Romney's home. He had been struggling with state and local regulations. He couldn't get help from anyone in government to break the deadlock.

Lynch met him on a plane. Within days, New Hampshire state officials were helping him move north of the border. They even helped him scout for a location.

If you have a governor who has a background in finance and private equity, including venture capital, you would hope that the state would see some benefit from it. Here, too, the voters were to be disappointed. According to the quarterly "Money Tree" venture capital report from PricewaterhouseCoopers, the accounting firm, during the Romney years Massachusetts attracted 12% of all venture capital money invested in new companies around America. That was just one percentage point above the average for the past two decades.

The state actually saw its share decline when it came to venture capital directed toward new biotech companies – a key area on which Massachusetts had been depending for growth. During the Romney years, the state got 18% of U.S. venture funding for biotech companies. Under his successor Deval Patrick (a Democrat) it has been 21%.

On the Road

When Romney ran for governor, he had promised that he would travel tirelessly around the country and the world – "outside Massachusetts, outside of our country" – to promote the state. Voters imagined him jetting from Cincinnati to Singapore, from New York to New Delhi, marketing Massachusetts and wooing investors and companies to the Bay State. "Mitt's said…that he'll be the state's top salesman," insisted Eric Fehrnstrom to the Boston Globe days after the election in 2002.

As they would discover over the next four years, getting Mitt Romney to travel out of the state wouldn't be a problem. The governor was frequently on the road. This was especially true after the 2004 elections. If he was trying to promote the state to big businesses and potential investors, however, he seemed to be going to the oddest places. The governor spent an awful lot of his time in states like Iowa, South Carolina, and Michigan. They had little economic importance to Massachusetts, but a great deal of political importance in the 2008 race for the Republican presidential nomination. They held early primaries or caucuses.

While there, Romney spent much of his time meeting local Republican activists. It hardly sounded like he was talking up his home state, either. Instead he seemed to relish in making Massachusetts sound as bad as possible.

In his home state, he said, he was like "a cattle-rancher at a vegetarian convention," and "a red dot in a blue state." He played up to the caricatures of Massachusetts as an oddball, far-left, moon-bat country, a strange land peopled with Kennedys and Kerrys and other out of touch "liberals." He took to mocking the city where he was nominally the head of the state, calling staid Boston "San Francisco East."

He derided the Massachusetts congressional delegation

for its "lack of political muscle" in Washington, made fun of the physical appearance of the state's junior Senator, John Kerry, and, reported my Boston Herald colleague Maggie Mulvihill, also made disparaging jokes about the state's organized crime, and about cost overruns at the "Big Dig" transportation project in Boston. (A Romney campaign commercial in Iowa a few years later, in 2007, even presented the governor's time in Massachusetts as if it had been a tour of duty in hostile territory, boasting he had been a conservative in "the toughest place.")

"He is using humor to disassociate himself from his own state," James Thurber, a politics professor at the American University in Washington, D.C., told Mulvihill in October, 2005. "It is state deprecating…It sounds like he has written off Massachusetts."

"Instead of serving as the Commonwealth's number one salesperson to encourage firms to locate in the state, he tended to poke fun at the state," Brian Gilmore, at the Associated Industries of Massachusetts, told the Globe. The AIM represented 7,600 Massachusetts businesses.

"It reinforces the perception that we're a difficult place to do business," he added. "We have a perception problem in the national marketplace – why add fuel to that?"

Romney's disparaging remarks were in sharp contrast to the tone he had set when he had run for governor. "I don't think people begin to understand what motivates me to run for office," he had said in 2002. "I really do want to make a difference. I believe Massachusetts is in trouble, and I think I can help."

You have to wonder what the audiences in places like Iowa and South Carolina thought of these remarks. If Romney had so little respect for Massachusetts, what was he doing as its governor?

His national Dissing Massachusetts tour took up increasing amounts of his time while he was still nominally in office.

Romney was absent from Massachusetts for 49 days in 2004, according to a report in the Boston Herald in December of that year. No comprehensive number was published for 2005, but the Boston Globe reported that year that he made nearly thirty trips out of the state, several of them for substantial periods. He was in Utah alone for 11 days. His trips included visits to New Hampshire, Iowa, South Carolina, Michigan and Florida – all key early states in the 2008 race for the Republican nomination.

When torrential rain and severe flooding hit Massachusetts in October, 2005, Romney was down in North Carolina, speaking to a fund-raiser there.

The Herald noted that during the year, his state campaign account had racked up more than $300,000 in traveling expenses on trips lasting a total of nearly fifty days.

Even a few state Republicans began to voice concerns. In October, 2005 Christine Cedrone, a Republican state committeewoman from Boston, told the Globe that Romney's absences were hurting. "I would like to see our governor be governor," she said. Kerry Healey, his lieutenant governor, was left insisting Romney could still govern effectively while on the road. "Being governor is something he can do, and he can lead, from here or wherever he is traveling and representing our state," she told the Worcester Telegram & Gazette in December, 2005.

By early 2006, Romney's absences had already become a pointed joke back home. At the annual St. Patrick's Day brunch in South Boston in March, the other politicians ribbed Romney about it. Romney joined in, thanking his hosts for the invitation, and joking that it was fortunate he happened to be in Massachusetts for the brunch.

The joke was on the Bay State voters. They were paying hundreds of thousands of dollars for Mitt Romney's security detail as their governor traveled around the country to states that could help his political ambitions rather than their economy.

Romney's absences in 2006, his final year in office, were of a different order. This was when he was serving as chairman of the Republican Governors' Association, and laying the groundwork for his presidential run. The Boston Globe, in official reports requisitioned from the State House, found Romney had been out of the state on a staggering 219 days in 2006, or four days in seven.

Let's do the math. He was out of the state for 49 days in 2004, at least 50 in 2005, and 219 in 2006. That takes us to around 320. The true figure in 2005 was probably higher. And we haven't even counted any days from 2003. In total, Romney may have been out of the state for the equivalent of a year of his term. I remember we used to joke at the Herald about the absentee governor. Friends in Boston – not, to be fair, political supporters of Romney – played a game called "Where's Mitt?" Sarah Palin has been panned for walking out of her job as governor of Alaska after only two and a half years. At least she resigned.

For many in Massachusetts, Romney's swift abandonment of the state was a big disappointment. They were left wondering aloud what might have been. As AIM's Brian Gilmore later put it in *The Real Romney*, many pondered "what Romney might have accomplished as governor had he focused his efforts more steadily on state policy leadership."

It is easy and tempting for a Republican governor who has disappointed expectations to blame his state's entrenched Democratic and liberal vested interests. There is something to it. However, it ignores everything we know about public leadership, and it makes a weak argument for the White House. Governors, like presidents, enjoy broad power to set the agenda and use the 'bully pulpit' to move the debate. They have powers of patronage and influence. Even in a heavily Democratic state like Massachusetts, a Republican governor can do a lot to change public opinion. Bill Weld, a decade earlier, had been very effective.

This excuse also misrepresents Massachusetts politics. The state is heavily dominated by one party, but that is not the same as saying it is as 'liberal' as its reputation would suggest. Independent voters in Massachusetts heavily outnumber registered Democrats. According to the Secretary of State's office, in October, 2002, when Romney was elected, there were 1.9 million independent voters compared to 1.4 million registered Democrats. Many state elections are simply uncontested. Political ambitions are all funneled through the Democratic party, but it is a broad church. It contains a lot of moderates and even conservatives. Most of Massachusetts is very suburban. It's a state of middle-class commuters, soccer practice, and cookouts in summer. Many prominent Democrats led the charge for charter schools and school choice back in the 1990s. Many Democrats opposed gay marriage when the Supreme Judicial Court first ruled in favor in 2003. There are very liberal pockets in the state, of course, such as college towns like Cambridge. But they are in the minority.

The argument that Mitt Romney couldn't change Massachusetts because it was just too liberal also has another weakness: If that were really the case, how come he got elected? Are we to believe it was his legendary charisma and charm? Massachusetts elected Republican governors four times in a row – once, in 1994, in a 71% landslide. In 2010, Massachusetts voters elected a Republican senator, Scott Brown, and he has a reasonable chance of being re-elected in 2012. In the past 20 years, the only time when the state has lacked a Republican statewide elected official has been from 2007 through 2009 – in the immediate aftermath of Mitt Romney's term of office.

People on Beacon Hill believe Romney quickly tired of the difficulties of politics there. He had meager interest in the politicians, and spent little time getting to know them. Politics is about back-slapping and back-scratching, especially in a town like Boston, and Romney didn't take much interest in either. He brought in his own team, including some of his traveling Mormon entourage, and stuck with them. They were considered, on Beacon Hill, a group apart. "A frequent complaint was that Romney, unlike previous Republican governors, rarely made an effort to develop meaningful relationships with the rank and file," wrote Kranish and Helman in *The Real Romney*. While at the Herald I frequently spoke to politicians on Beacon Hill. I noted how rarely they mentioned the governor. He was seen like a constitutional monarch: Decorative, but distant. Tom Finneran, a Beacon Hill veteran and the Democratic Speaker of the House for the first half of Romney's term, contrasted Romney's reserve with that of his predecessor Bill Weld.

Romney didn't help his own case politically, either. During the 2004 elections, half way through his term, he chose two simultaneous and conflicting strategies.

On the one hand, with his eyes on national politics, Romney buddied up with the Bush-Cheney re-election campaign – just as it launched its brutal and highly personal campaign against its opponent, Massachusetts senator John Kerry. At times Bush seemed to be running not just against Kerry but against his state as well. "What do you expect from a senator from Massachusetts?" asked the president with a smirk at one point. (Imagine any other state's name in that sentence.)

On the other hand, Romney also launched an aggressive bid to try to win more Republican seats on Beacon Hill in the state elections. This meant, of course, taking on lots of incumbents. Romney recruited a huge slate of candidates and then threw himself into the campaign. In some races the tone became negative.

In the national election, John Kerry carried Massachusetts in a landslide, nearly two to one. The Bush effect rubbed off on the state elections. Romney's Republicans lost seats. The governor was weakened, and he had alienated the Democrats as well. When he tried appealing to bipartisanship a few weeks later, and said he wanted to get together with people on both sides to talk about health insurance reform, it was a tough sell. "This administration hasn't been willing to work with anyone," Christine Canavan, the House vice-chairwoman on health care, told the Globe: "I just came out of a campaign where the man was trying to make sure I wasn't here anymore."

Romney's conclusion? He had given too much of himself to others, including the state GOP, he told the Boston Globe editorial board a few weeks later. "From now on," he told them, "it's me-me-me."

On Beacon Hill

Romney's signature success as governor was his dramatic reform to the state's healthcare system. Massachusetts, of course, became the first state in the country to bring in near-universal healthcare. The reform, contrary to later criticisms during the Republican primaries, has worked pretty well and most people are happy with it. Romney played an important role and deserves real credit. Yet there was much more to it behind the scenes. On the day Romney signed the bill into law, in a big ceremony at Faneuil Hall, my colleague Shelly Cohen, the Opinion editor of the Boston Herald, revealed some of the back story:

"Civic leaders like Peter Meade of Blue Cross and Jack Connors, chairman of the [hospitals non-profit] Partners board, had a helluva lot more to do with passage of the health-care bill by breaking the legislative logjam than Romney ever did," she wrote. "But since neither is running for office they haven't scheduled any press interviews on the subject. (They personify that ancient bit of wisdom that there's no end to what you can accomplish if you don't care who gets the credit.)"

Cohen added that if Romney really wanted to find out how "his" law worked out when it took effect in 2007, "he'll have to peek in from New Hampshire or Iowa or wherever he's campaigning…Not to worry, we'll drop him a line."

The Herald, it should be added, is the conservative paper in Boston. It had supported Romney in 2002.

Beyond healthcare, what were Romney's other achievements?

He came to office during a crunch caused by the state recession in 2000-2. He has since claimed that he closed a gap of around $3 billion, and did so without raising taxes. According to a report in the Globe, he told a group in Michigan in March, 2005, that he "went after waste, inefficiency, duplication, and patronage."

Romney deserves recognition for making some sensible cuts and achieving some worthwhile efficiencies. But the reality is not quite as he sells it.

Factcheck.org points out that about $1.3 billion of the budget gap was simply closed by a surge in capital gains receipts during the year. Receipts were up because the stock market recovered. In 2003 the U.S. stock market jumped more than 20 percent. Another $500 billion came from the federal government, in the form of extra Medicaid funding. The real gap that had to be closed was only about $1.2 billion, it concluded.

Some of that came from cutting local aid to cities and towns. Cities and towns rarely have much fat in their budgets, as they provide essential services. And most are prevented by law from raising taxes. This move simply passed on the burden to them.

Michael Widmer, the nonpartisan head of the Massachusetts Taxpayers Foundation, was unimpressed. Some of Romney's reforms were good, he countered, but "they have no connection to the closing of the (budget) gap," he told the Globe in October, 2005. "No reform has saved any meaningful money. It's all on the margins."

Romney has said he didn't raise "taxes," but that depends on how you look at it. Instead he raised "fees" for various government services, and eliminated tax "loopholes."(A loophole, he later explained, was "where someone uses a provision of the tax code in a way it was not intended to be used.") The Boston Globe put the total increase at $515 million. Factcheck.org, citing the Massachusetts Taxpayers' Foundation, put it at $750 million. The Romney campaign in January 2012 said it had only been $434 million.

The estimates worked out to an increase in state revenue of between $67 and $118 per person.

While raising fees and closing loopholes, reported the Pioneer Institute, Mitt Romney also presided over a massive – and probably avoidable – hike in unemployment taxes.

The state's $2 billion-a-year unemployment insurance program was in crisis and nearly insolvent when he took office. And no wonder: The system, noted the institute, was "rife with abuse." Certain industries could game it quite easily, driving up costs for everyone else. The self-employed could actually collect generous benefits each year by just laying themselves off when their slow season came around. Romney proposed some reforms, but failed to follow through on them. In the end, noted Pioneer, he didn't even try to veto a bill that hiked the taxes while instituting only minimal reforms. "Between 2003 and 2005, the average UI [Unemployment Insurance] taxes paid by a typical Massachusetts company almost doubled," the think-tank reported. By 2006 the average business was paying $629 a year per employee – more than twice the national average. It was precisely the kind of issue that had been calling out for smart leadership by a conservative who could master the details.

The year before Romney became governor, Massachusetts ranked 12th in America in terms of its tax climate for business, according to the non-partisan Tax Foundation in Washington, D.C. When Romney left it ranked…34th. In 2002, the year before Romney took over, the average Massachusetts citizen paid $2,976 in state and local taxes, according to the Tax Foundation's annual survey. In 2006, after four years of an administration that he would later call "severely conservative," that had risen to $3,705. A 25% increase.

Romney has reasonably criticized the Obama administration for presiding over a monumental increase in America's national debt. But what was his own legacy?

In 2002, shortly before Romney was elected, the U.S. Census says Massachusetts state debts amounted to $45 billon. In 2006, shortly before he left, these had risen to $64 billion. That was a 42% increase. By 2007, according to the Massachusetts state government, the state had one of the highest debt levels per person in America. If Romney didn't cause it, he didn't cure it either.

What had the state received for all that debt? Drive out of Boston in any direction and the chances are you will soon come across rusting bridges and crumbling roads. In March, 2007, less than three months after Romney left office, the state's Transportation Finance Commission revealed the entire system was in crisis, needing billions in urgent repairs. In 2008, Geoffrey Beckwith, executive director of the Massachusetts Municipal Association, pleaded with state legislators to support an emergency $3 billion bond issue. He pointed out that by federal standards 52% of the state's bridges were now either "structurally deficient" or "functionally obsolete." In other words, just over half were falling apart. During a debate in New Hampshire in June, 2007, Romney quoted an oilman who said America's oil refineries were so run-down they were "rust, with paint holding them up." By then the same was true of some of the bridges in Massachusetts. The Storrow Drive tunnel under Boston was "literally falling apart,"

Mass. Taxpayers' Michael Widmer told the Herald in March, 2007, barely three months after Romney had left office. He called the situation "disgraceful." The historic Longfellow Bridge between Boston and Cambridge was in such bad shape that in 2008 it had to be closed for Boston's famous Fourth of July firework celebrations. Inspections found it simply unsafe for spectators to stand on.

Meanwhile the state's transportation finances were so badly messed up, the Pioneer Institute discovered, that Massachusetts was issuing 20-year bonds so it could pay people to cut the grass along the sides of the highways.

These problems had grown up over decades, not years. Romney didn't cause them. Yet he certainly didn't fix them either. These are hardly ideological matters where you might expect a partisan stalemate, either. They are obvious "turnaround" tasks. His Democratic successor, Deval Patrick, pushed through emergency repair plans to try to address some of the worst damage.

Elsewhere, too, "waste, inefficiency, duplication, and patronage" seemed to defy the Romney touch. In 2005, for example, he brought in a special "turnaround" expert to fix the troubled State Medical Examiner's office. When Romney left office, more than two years later, the department was still in such disarray that bodies were piled up in a refrigerated truck out back. In May, 2007, Governor Patrick was forced to step in after the department actually lost a body.

Romney also left behind a state where public payrolls were riddled with unchecked abuse, from transport to pensions to police overtime. The net result was costing taxpayers millions a year.

An investigation by the Boston Globe in 2007 found hundreds of state cops abusing the overtime system and the arcane regulations on traffic details to take home six figure incomes. Two dozen made more than $200,000 a year. The Herald revealed hundreds of cases of featherbedding across state government, with thousands earning six-figure incomes. It had all been going on right under Romney's nose. He certainly didn't cause it. It had been going on for years. But he didn't stop it, or expose it, either.

Maybe some of these things come with the territory when you govern a state, especially a complex one like Massachusetts. But they scarcely fit the hands-on, "turnaround" image.

Furthermore, Romney wasn't above trying a little patronage of his own at the taxpayers' expense. Barely a month before he was due to leave office, he tried to slip his close adviser Eric Fehrnstrom into a cozy part-time job that would have ended up costing Massachusetts taxpayers hundreds of thousands of dollars in extra pension benefits.

The news item sounded innocent enough. It was late November, 2006: The day before Thanksgiving. The administration had appointed Fehrnstrom as the new member to the housing authority of Brookline, an upscale suburb just west of Boston. The post only paid $5,000 a year. Who cared?

The devil was in the details. In Massachusetts, anyone who wants to qualify for a lucrative state pension needs to rack up ten years' service in the public sector. By November, 2006, Fehrnstrom only had eight, and he was due to leave office with Romney in a matter of weeks.

The Brookline post, due to last five years, would have put him over the top. And it would pay out, big time – far bigger than the $5,000 salary. A Massachusetts state pension isn't tied to your last salary. It's tied to your salary for your three highest-earning years. Fehrnstrom was making $160,000 a year as Romney's spokesman. The Brookline post would also have meant he would become entitled to state health care and life insurance benefits, and Medicare-plus insurance over 65.

If there was any doubt in the matter, consider the timing of the move. As anyone in politics or public relations knows, the day before Thanksgiving is when you try to slip things by the press and the public. Everyone is out of town. No one is watching.

Romney was traveling in Florida at the time. His spokesman initially said he couldn't be reached.

When the Boston Globe caught the news item, Fehrnstrom, and then Romney, pleaded innocence. It had simply never occurred to them that Fehrnstrom's non-job in Brookline would have secured him a full pension, they said.

Mitt Romney, the anti-patronage businessman who prided himself on the mastery of details, pleaded ignorance. "I don't know at this point what the pension implications are," Romney told the Boston Globe. "I don't know whether [Fehrnstrom] does or anyone else does."

Michael Travaglini, head of the state pension board, wasn't buying it. "This smacks of collusion," he told the Globe. "Mr. Fehrnstrom shopped around for a position that would allow him to be eligible for a pension. And by appointing him to the housing board, the governor is complicit. You don't need a forensic accountant to connect the dots." After the heat became too much for Romney, Fehrnstrom pulled out – and in a Nixonian moment said the whole affair had been unjustly used by Mitt Romney's opponents to make "unwarranted attacks."

Romney and Fehrnstrom tried their stunt with the pension just two weeks after the governor had used emergency powers to cut pay for state social workers making $11 an hour.

In the 2006 elections Romney's would-be Republican successor, his lieutenant governor Kerry Healey, got crushed in a landslide by her Democratic rival. The old Bill Weld Republican coalition, which had united Massachusetts Republicans, fiscal conservatives, moderates and independents through four elections, collapsed. Many moderates and independents switched to the Democratic candidate, Deval Patrick, or to independent businessman Christy Mihos, instead. Romney barely lifted a finger to campaign for Healey. A few weeks before the election, he disloyally predicted on national television that she would lose. She had helped him a lot during his 2002 election and his term, but the favor was scarcely returned.

While Romney was governor, 30,000 Massachusetts Republican voters switched their registration to something else. He left the party with just 12.5% of registered voters.

When Mitt Romney launched his bid for president, days after leaving office, he found many state GOP stalwarts turned their backs. Former governor Paul Cellucci endorsed Rudy Giuliani. So did three of the state's five Republican state senators, the Globe reported. Others went for John McCain. So did the editorial board of the Herald – a point McCain raised at a key moment in a debate. When the New Hampshire primary rolled around a year later, McCain beat Romney by 37% to 31%, effectively ending Romney's run. Four years later, he still couldn't get above 39%. In the intervening years he'd gained just 20,000 extra votes. To many, it must have felt like karma.

3

THE TRUTH ABOUT BAIN CAPITAL

If there is one thing everyone seems to agree on, it's that Mitt Romney was a spectacular success in business.

Romney was "a brilliant businessman," according to the New York Times' David Brooks. He was "coolly brilliant," agreed his biographers, Kranish and Helman. Critics may say he was an evil genius who closed down companies and laid off workers. Supporters may say he was an investment genius who made companies more efficient and produced superb returns for investors. But no one seems to question his success at what he did.

Romney has made his record in business a key point in his election campaign. "Our president doesn't understand how the economy works," he told an MSNBC presidential debate in September, 2011. "I do, because I've lived in it." His twenty-five years' experience, "succeeding, failing, competing around the world," he said, gave him "the capacity to help get this economy going again...to put together a plan to help restructure the basis of America's economic foundation so we can create jobs again, good jobs, and compete with anyone in the world."

But what was that experience? What does his business career tell us about Romney? And was he really as good as the reports claim?

Mitt Romney's most important job was as the chief executive officer of a private equity company, Bain Capital, from 1984 to 1998 inclusive. That's where he made his wealth and his reputation.

What is private equity? It's a business that buys companies with borrowed money and then tries to sell them for a profit. It's that simple. A private equity manager does to companies what a real estate speculator does to houses: He buys them with a small deposit and a big mortgage, fixes them up, and then sells them. Sometimes, if the market is really roaring, he doesn't even need to fix them up. As Romney wrote in *Turnaround*, "We would invest in these underperforming companies, using the equivalent of a mortgage to leverage up our investment. Then we would go to work to help management make their businesses more successful." He added, in an unguarded moment: "I never actually ran one of our investments; that was left to management."

Most accounts in the media say that Romney and his firm were extraordinarily successful – that when it came to finding companies with potential, they had the golden touch.

Published reports cite fantastic performance figures. Some media reports say the firm earned "50% to 80% a year" for investors over fifteen years. *The Real Romney* cites reports that put the figure even higher, at an incredible 88% a year. The American Enterprise Institute think-tank in Washington, D.C., went even further than that. In a glowing profile of Mitt Romney published in its magazine, The American, in 2006, it claimed: "During the 14 years

Romney headed Bain Capital, the firm's average annual internal rate of return on realized investments was a staggering 113 percent." The magazine added: "At that growth rate, a hypothetical $1,000 investment would grow to $39.6 million before fees. Few, if any, VC firms have ever matched Bain Capital's performance under Mitt Romney."

These are amazing numbers.

Alas, they are too amazing.

My job involves writing a lot about superstar investment managers. I've met many over the years. I view them like chess grandmasters – rare, fascinating geniuses. But I had never heard of a manager, or a firm, producing returns of 88% a year – let alone 113% – over fourteen or fifteen years. Not even in a boom. I decided to do a little digging.

The first thing to know about private equity is that the industry operates behind closed doors. Private equity firms don't comment on their investment returns in public. Academic researchers have to sign the most stringent anti-disclosure forms in order to get access to data. "Private equity funds," warns the Harvard Business School overview of its own course on the subject, "jealously guard their privacy." Brian Cheffins and John Armour, two experts at Cambridge University, say that "privacy has been a hallmark of private equity," and add that big firms like Bain Capital operate "as secretive partnerships."

So assessing the firm's investment performance is not as simple as assessing that of a mutual fund, or a publicly-traded stock. The numbers aren't straightforward or public. We have to deal with partial information, some assumptions, and some intelligent guesswork.

The best overall account of Bain Capital's performance under Mitt Romney is a prospectus produced in 2000 by Wall Street's Deutsche Bank as it sought to raise money for a new fund. This is the main source relied on by the Wall Street Journal, the Los Angeles Times, the Boston Globe, and other publications. It's the one cited by the Romney campaign itself when discussing his record.

It tells a story. And one of the first things you notice is that a few things don't add up. For example, the prospectus shows that Bain Capital's clients invested about $900 million during Romney's fifteen year tenure. But if you invested $900 million in steady amounts over fifteen years and earned "80%" a year, by the end you would have about $900 *billion*. If you earned "113%" a year, you would end up with about $9 *trillion* – or nearly two-thirds of the size of the U.S. economy's annual output. Such are the miracles of compound interest. Bain Capital is a wealthy company. But if it now owned two-thirds of the nation's annual economic output, I think we might have heard.

Professor Ludovic Phalippou at Oxford University's business school, a leading expert on private equity, has a simple verdict for some of the sky-high figures being bandied about. They are, he says, "absurd."

"These returns...are vastly overstated," he told me. "The 'star' returns are overstated, sometimes to absurd magnitudes like in the case of the 80% of Bain." Such numbers, he said, bear little relation to what investors actually earned.

Why? Put simply, there are lots of ways of calculating annual rates of return for an investment fund. Should you use a geometric average or an arithmetic one? Time-weighted rates of return, or dollar-weighted? Should you calculate your returns based on all the money committed to the funds, or just the money actually invested? Should you use simple returns, or annualized ones? Gross or net? Private equity managers and Wall Street bankers, for obvious reasons, tend to prefer numbers that make them look best.

To take one example: In 1996, Bain Capital bought consumer credit company Experian for about $80 million and then sold it for about $250 million. To you or me this would count as a 200% gain: Bain Capital trebled its money. But according to the Deutsche Bank prospectus, this deal had an "implied annualized internal rate of return" of "6,636%." The reason? The deal went through in seven weeks. On an annualized basis, it's amazing. But that's only relevant to investors if Bain Capital were able to come up with a string of identical deals for a full year.

Or try this: Imagine you hire your brother-in-law for a year to manage some of your money, much as people hire Bain Capital. Let's say you give him $100.

On the first day he spends $1 of that money buying a bag of muffins and takes it to his office, where he sells the muffins to coworkers for $2. He then does nothing for the rest of the year.

When you meet to settle accounts, your brother-in-law hands you back your original $100 investment, plus your $1 profit. You would hardly be impressed at his investment success. But he could tell you, quite truthfully, that he had produced an "average internal rate of return" on his "realized investments" of 100%. He had one realized investment. The return was 100%.

If you think that's crazy, try this. Imagine the same scenario, but in this case he buys two bags of muffins, each for $1. On the first day he sells the muffins from one bag to coworkers for $2. On the second day the company starts offering free muffins in the cafeteria. No one wants your brother-in-law's muffins any more. He puts the second bag in the freezer, where it sits for the rest of the year, unsold and uneaten.

In this case when you meet up he hands you back your original $100 plus a bag of frozen muffins. No loss, no gain. The $1 profit made on the first bag of muffins is offset by the $1 wasted on the second bag. Yet he can still boast of an "average internal rate of return on realized investments" of 100%. He made two investments. The first was "realized" when he sold the muffins. On that investment he made a 100% return. The second investment – the second bag of muffins – never got sold. He is still carrying it on the books at its historical cost, $1. So far, there has been no loss.

Wall Street is full of stuff like this. Funds can cash in on the best investments early to boost the internal rate of return. They delay selling the bad investments as long as possible. They may never sell them at all. Their performance numbers can be even crazier than the ones here. That bag of muffins sold on the first day? On Wall Street, the rate of return would be annualized. A return of 100% achieved in one day, compounded for a full year, is an astronomical number with about 90 zeros on the end. Let's call it all the money in the world, and then some.

So how did Bain Capital really do under Mitt Romney?

From 1984 through the end of 1998, the Wall Street prospectus shows, Bain Capital's investors put in about $900 million, and the firm's investments produced gains of about $2.4 billion. This may understate the final total a little, as some investments hadn't fully matured. Nonetheless it's the best figure we have, and the one most widely relied upon by all sides.

How's that?

Hmmm.

I asked Vanguard, the low-cost mutual fund company, how much investors would have made from 1984 through 1998 if they had just dollar-cost averaged $900 million into a basic U.S. stock index fund.

Their response: About $3.5 billion. That's $1 billion *more* than Bain Capital's profits.

No, i's not an apples-to-apples comparison. It's important to make that clear. There are several other factors that we need to include: More about them in a moment. But it's context. The most far-fetched estimates of Mitt Romney's investment performance should be tossed aside. They're nonsense.

Professor Phalippou says that in private equity the average dollar is invested for about four years. If that was the case at Bain Capital, it would mean the annual returns on investment from 1984 to 1998 were about 40%.

But a source with direct knowledge of Bain Capital's investments during the Romney years says that its investment dollars were tied up for longer, "about to five or seven years." If that was the case, the returns come down to a more modest 20% to 30% a year.

We don't know the precise figure, and they will always be subject to some debate. But these are the ballpark numbers.

Now let's look at the context.

Private equity, as mentioned earlier, is like real estate investment. Mitt Romney and his team bought companies with the equivalent of a mortgage, fixed them up, and then tried to sell them for a profit.

Real estate speculation certainly involves skill. You need to have a network that gets you access to the best deals and the right financing. You have to be able to negotiate well. You have to get tough with contractors. You have to have judgment. You will not do very well if you buy homes on the wrong side of town, or if you pay too much.

These are all important. However, as most people now know, the most important skill of a successful real estate speculator isn't any of the above.

It's timing.

Someone who speculated on real estate in Las Vegas between 2000 and 2005 made a fortune. Someone who bought the same homes in 2005 and tried to speculate over the next five years lost a fortune. Same homes. Same streets. Same town. Very different result.

That's because Las Vegas was in a booming market in the first half of last decade, and it was in a crashing market in the second half. For an investor or speculator, rising and falling markets are more important than anything else. If real estate prices are skyrocketing and the banks are handing out cheap loans, you do not need to be very skillful to do well. Many Las Vegas real estate speculators made a fortune early last decade, but we are not trawling their ranks for presidential candidates.

Mitt Romney got the call from Bill Bain to set up Bain Capital in 1983. At the time Romney was a young 36-year-old partner at Bain & Co., the strategy consultancy. Setting up a private equity company was not his idea. It was Bain's. According to several accounts, Romney took a lot of persuading to make the jump. He thought the new venture sounded too risky. In the end, after lots of assurances, he agreed to take it on. He ran Bain Capital until the start of 1999. Then he left to take over the troubled Salt Lake City Olympics.

Those fifteen years would turn out, in hindsight, to be the most spectacular years in history to be in private equity – the equivalent of the recent real estate bubble in Las Vegas. They happened to coincide with the greatest bull market in the history of the U.S. stock market.

As Mitt Romney later admitted, according to *The Real Romney*, "I was in the investment business during the most robust years in the history of investments."

Stock prices soared. The Dow Jones Industrial Average rose more than sevenfold. When you include dividends, Wall Street research company MSCI reports that a passive investor who just invested across the whole market increased his money twelvefold during that time.

And that wasn't all. As Mitt Romney said, Bain Capital didn't just buy companies. It bought them with borrowed money. And here it got a second, wonderful piece of news. The cost of debt – like the cost of mortgages for a real estate speculator – collapsed. Over this period prime lending rates fell from 12% to about 8%, according to the Federal Reserve. The interest rate on corporate bonds halved.

So for the fifteen years that Romney was at Bain Capital, it got cheaper and cheaper and cheaper to borrow money to buy stocks that just went up and up and up. There was, in short, never a better moment in human history to borrow money and use it to buy U.S. companies.

According to MSCI, during those years you could have just picked stocks randomly out of the newspaper, gone fishing, and earned an average of about 20% a year. No Harvard MBAs. No investment whizz-kids. No Mitt Romney. A dart board, a copy of the stock prices page of the Wall Street Journal, and a fishing rod. Twenty percent a year.

What if you'd bought those stocks with debt, like Bain Capital? You'd have earned a lot more.

Borrowing 50% of your investment dollars, at corporate interest rates, would have sent your annual returns zooming to nearly 30%. Borrowing two-thirds of your investment would have sent them up to around 35% a year.

In other words, if you had borrowed a lot of money during these years and just bought a random collection of U.S. stocks picked out of the paper, you'd have earned annual investment returns in the same ballpark as those likely earned by Bain Capital under Mitt Romney.

Or, to put it another way: The lion's share of Romney's investment returns had nothing to do with skill at finding the right underperforming companies, or from making operational improvements. They were due to timing and debt. The firm was basically buying U.S. stocks with borrowed money at the perfect moment in history.

Oh, and there's another thing.

These figures you hear about Bain Capital's investment returns? They are *gross* – before fees.

When I first realized that, I couldn't believe it. After all, every mutual fund quotes its figures net of fees. So does every hedge fund I know.

But there it is, a little footnote at the bottom of the

prospectus: Bain Capital returns are quoted "Before expenses, fees and General Partner carried interest [i.e., Bain Capital's share]."

Fees are the big story on Wall Street. Indeed they are the subject of the oldest joke there. It features a visitor from out of town who is being shown around by a friend at a big Wall Street bank. The friend proudly points out all the yachts in the harbor owned by the brokers, money managers and so on. At the end the visitor innocently asks: "And where are the customers' yachts?"

I've long argued that Wall Street is one of the least capitalist places in the world. Nowhere else do the owners of capital – the investors – hand over so much of their money to the workers. Karl Marx wouldn't believe his eyes.

And if Wall Street represents the triumph of labor (loosely defined) over capital, those in private equity are the Revolutionary Front. The fees they charge are somewhere between heroic and astronomical. Bain Capital charged investors between 1.5% to 2% of their money each year, just for managing it. They took another 20% of any profits. Simple math will tell you that over the course of fifteen years, based on the information we have about the size of the investment funds, Bain Capital probably pocketed more than $500 million in fees – quite possibly a lot more. (Oxford's Phalippou says the industry norm works out at about 7% of assets a year, including a lot of obscure fees the clients usually overlook.)

Once you deduct these fees, you realize that during a fifteen year period Mitt Romney's investors put in about $900 million and may have made gains of only $1.9 billion. If their average dollar was invested for five to seven years, that would work out, net, at around 18% to 25% a year.

That compares with 20% just from investing blindly across the market, without any debt, and going fishing.

Naturally, very few people took out gigantic mortgages in the early 1980s and used the money to buy stocks. For an ordinary person the costs and legal difficulties of doing so would have been prohibitive. And their necks would be on the line if it went the wrong way. Debt can bring higher returns, but it also means higher risk. Few people want to take a massive gamble in this way with their own money.

But if you work on Wall Street, including at a private equity company like Bain Capital, you have one big advantage over everyone else. You get to gamble with other people's money.

The United States has generous "walk away" corporate bankruptcy rules. They were designed, back in the past, so that legitimate businessmen who failed in a business could get back on their feet and try again.

For people in private equity, when an investment goes bad, they just write it off. They never end up on the hook for the bad debts. They are like Bill Murray's weatherman in Groundhog Day. They can behave as recklessly as they like and it won't matter. Tomorrow they can start again as if nothing happened. This lets them take big risks.

There was the case of Dade International, a medical diagnostics business based in Illinois that Bain Capital bought from Baxter International. Bain put down $27 million, alongside some other investors, to buy the company, and pocketed $230 million. Meanwhile, according to published accounts, Dade racked up $1.6 billion in debt. A few years later, in 2002, the company laid off 1,700 workers and had to go through bankruptcy protection.

Or there was GS Steel. This is a steel company that Bain Capital owned which collapsed in 2002. About 750 workers lost their jobs. Romney has faced criticism on this from Republicans and Democrats alike. He points out in his defense that he had left Bain Capital when GS Steel closed down. And he points out that the company was hit very hard by a worldwide slump in the steel business, which was neither his fault, nor that of Bain Capital.

Both may be fair points. But what really matters is that

Bain Capital effectively took a big mortgage equity withdrawal on GS Steel soon after buying it in the mid-1990s – when Romney was still there. In two years, the company said in public filings, GS Steel borrowed at least $250 million. The company paid out some of that in dividends to Bain Capital. That vastly boosted the company's returns.

When the industry slump hit later, there was no way to get that money back.

Bain Capital made an annualized return of more than 400% on its small GS Steel investment, Wall Street documents show. Banks and bondholders lost money. (And so did the government. News service Reuters reported in January, 2012 that the federal government's pension guarantee fund had to pay $44 million to bail out the company's pension fund.) None of the millions Bain Capital had taken out of the company earlier was ever clawed back. There was no way to do so.

"I'm a guy who has lived in the world of business," Mitt Romney boasted during a Republican debate in Arizona in February, 2012, as he sought to put down Rick Santorum's lack of experience. "If you don't balance your budget in business," Romney added, "you go out of business." Except it was the creditors, and others, who went out of business. Not Bain Capital.

According to the Wall Street Journal analysis in January, 2012, about 22% of the companies Bain Capital bought – more than one in five – either ended up in Chapter 11, or closed their doors, in the eight-year period after Bain Capital bought them. (Bain Capital challenged the point.)

It's amazing what risks you can take if you don't have to bear the consequences. For example, Wall Street documents show Bain Capital made spectacular "internal rates of return" of 1,100% on one of its earliest deals under Mitt Romney, Accuride, which it bought in 1986 and sold a few years later. How do you earn returns that big? Easy: Debt.

Lots of it. According to newspaper reports at the time, Bain Capital put down just 3% of the purchase price. Most of the remaining $200 million it borrowed. The gamble worked out. If it hadn't? Too bad – for others.

What was the effect of this on the economy?

From 1982 to 1999, thanks in part to the boom in debt-backed takeovers by private equity companies such as Bain Capital, the debts of U.S. corporations quadrupled. In 1982 they had had pretty strong balance sheets. By 1999, says the Federal Reserve, their average debts were more than half their net worth – a postwar record.

Bain and Jobs

Imagine you overheard a coworker in the office canteen bragging that she had helped create "two million jobs" in America. Imagine furthermore that you asked her what she meant, and she answered: "Well, I've had all my money in a U.S. mutual fund for the past ten years. Over that time American companies have created about two million jobs."

You would probably not be very impressed by her claim to be a "job creator." It wouldn't make much difference if she added, "I didn't say I had created them all by myself, I just said I had helped create them." Everyone who invests in U.S. companies – who provides them with the risk capital they need – is helping them to grow and therefore create jobs. So is everyone who shops in an American store or buys an American product. But how much credit can we take for that? If your mutual funds own stock in Apple, can you say you helped invent the iPhone?

If your coworker wanted to take credit, she would need to show how she was actually involved in the management of the companies, and took risks or innovated to help create growth. Just investing doesn't cut it.

Mitt Romney likes to say that in his career at Bain

Capital he created businesses and jobs. "We helped create businesses that grew, that employed people," he said during a primary debate in Florida in January. "We helped start Staples, for instance. It employs 90,000 people...We were able to create thousands and thousands of jobs."

He has claimed that "net, net" he and Bain Capital have created or "helped create...over 100,000 jobs." In an interview with Time magazine in December, 2011, Romney said of Bain, "net-net, we created over 100,000 jobs." On Fox two weeks later he added that "in my former life we helped create over 100,000 jobs."

It's a line he's been using since he first ran for the Senate in 1994. According to a Boston Globe account in August of that year, Romney aired campaign commercials in which a narrator said, "Mitt Romney has spent his life building more than 20 businesses and helping to create more than 10,000 jobs...So when it comes to creating jobs, he's not just talk. He's done it."

Romney's critics have responded by trying to argue the opposite: That he's a "vulture capitalist" who lays people off and destroys companies.

Ted Kennedy successfully used this line against him during their 1994 Senate race, blaming Romney and Bain Capital for layoffs at a Midwestern paper company they owned.

Republican rival Mike Huckabee used it against him in the 2008 presidential race, memorably saying, "I want to be a president who reminds you of the guy you work with, not the guy who laid you off." In early 2012 Newt Gingrich leveled similar charges against him. As the former Speaker said during a presidential debate in South Carolina in January, "Bain Capital's model...was to take over a company and dramatically lever it, leave it with a great deal of debt, make it less likely to survive."

Barack Obama and the Democrats are making it a major issue of the campaign against Romney this time around, raising the issue of layoffs at companies that Bain Capital owned such as GS Steel and American Pad & Paper.

Most of the coverage of Bain Capital has focused on "jobs lost" versus "jobs gained" at companies in which Bain Capital invested.

There are several problems with this.

First, it's meaningless. If you go into a company that is going bust with 300 employees, and you manage to save it with 150 employees, have you created or destroyed jobs?

Second, why shouldn't companies lay people off? It is an unfortunate, but inevitable, consequence of growth and change. Why would we expect any company to employ more people than it needs? Unless we are willing to argue that a profitable company should keep hiring surplus workers until the profits are all used up, we must also accept that companies with surplus staff can legitimately let them go, even when the company is already profitable.

As for the debate about "offshoring": What a charade this is. Current law effectively *forces* companies to close their U.S. operations and source production in cheaper Third World countries like China instead. This lets them do an end-run around U.S. labor laws and environmental regulations. They can move production from a clean factory in Ohio to one in Asia that dumps poisonous chemicals in the river. They can lay off American workers who get good wages, benefits, and basic protections, and replace them with serfs working in conditions that, quite literally, drive them to suicide.

If the president or his party is pushing to change the laws to stop this behavior, I must have missed it. It's among the issues that neither party is discussing at all. On the contrary, the modern system that is usually termed "free trade" seems to be supported without question on both sides. It's pointless to blame companies for playing by stupid rules. So long as these rules remain in place, companies will take advantage of them. They will do so when they are owned by Bain Capital, just as they will do so when they are owned by public investors on the stock market.

Publicly-traded companies have a legal obligation to maximize profits for their investors. If the management doesn't use every legal maneuver to do so, someone else – including a private equity company – will take it over and do it instead.

If President Obama objects to offshoring, he should propose legislation to stop it.

Focusing on these sideshow issues has distracted people from the more important point: How much can Romney really claim to have created (or destroyed) any jobs at all?

Take the company for which Romney most frequently takes credit: Staples, the stationery chain. Bain Capital was an early stage investor. But when you study the record, which has been widely published, you find that Mitt Romney and Bain Capital really didn't provide very much.

They didn't come up with the deal. That was actually Bessemer Partners, a venture capital company in Boston. (In a funny twist of fate, one of Bessemer's founders, Chris Gabrieli, would later be a Democratic political opponent of Romney's.) It didn't provide much of the money: According to an account in the Boston Globe in October, 1994, Bain provided just $2.5 million of the $35 million that Staples raised when it started up. That's 7% of the money.

Bain Capital didn't come up with the business idea. Thomas Stemberg was the entrepreneur who thought it up. When he first pitched it to Bain Capital, according to multiple reports, Mitt Romney dismissed it. Romney and his team said companies didn't spend enough on stationery to make Stemberg's business idea attractive. Their source? They'd asked some CEOs how much their businesses spent on stationery. But Stemberg's brilliant insight was that CEOs didn't know the true figure, and that their businesses were spending far, far more on stationery than they realized.

Romney didn't get it. Stemberg had to explain it to him twice.

So the question isn't whether Staples has created jobs – it has. And it isn't whether it has put a lot of mom and pop stationers out of work. The real question is why we should take the company's success as a mark of Mitt Romney's personal genius.

Furthermore, he tries to have it both ways. When it suits him, Romney is willing to imply that he played a very active role at the companies in which he invested. At other times he implies the reverse.

During his campaign against Ted Kennedy in 1994, he frequently tried to take credit for Staples' success. Romney also boasted on that campaign that every company he had ever run had provided health insurance to all employees. Kennedy responded that Staples, for one, did not provide health insurance for its many part-time workers. Charlie Manning, Romney's spokesman, retorted that this was nothing to do with Romney, as he had very little involvement in the company after all. "He does not run Staples," Manning told the Boston Globe.

It turned out that when Romney was referring to the companies he had "run," he had meant just Bain Capital, the private equity partnership, and Bain & Co., the management consulting firm, where he had been briefly CEO. Of course, such lucrative firms almost always provide healthcare benefits for all their employees. It was an empty boast.

Romney himself in *Turnaround*, his book about the Salt Lake City Olympics, was astonishingly blunt about his actual experience. "I never actually ran one of our investments; that was left to management," he wrote. It was a remarkable statement. It didn't end there, either. In 1998, at the end of his private sector career, the Olympics organizers in Utah asked him to take over the Games there. He wrote in *Turnaround*, "I protested, 'I don't have any project management experience.' " So much for the twenty-five years as a hands-on executive.

It doesn't end there. Romney has frequently claimed that he was a "venture capitalist," helping to create new companies. But Bain Capital's main business was buying existing companies with debt. Some of its biggest profits came from a handful of quick deals – like the $160 million it made in 1996 by flipping Experian, a consumer credit company, in seven weeks. Bain and another private equity company bought Experian with about 10% down and 90% debt. They were looking for competitors to acquire. When their Wall Street bank put out feelers, they heard back from a British company that wanted to buy Experian instead. The offer came out of the blue. The Wall Street Journal called it "one of the quickest big hits in Wall Street history."

Lucky them. But no one can "turn around" a company in seven weeks. Bain Capital did nothing to change the company. Other big wins involved big "cash-out refis," such as GS Steel.

Mitt Romney likes to downplay that side of his business. "The idea of making a short-term profit actually doesn't really exist in business," he told voters in a CNN debate in South Carolina in January, 2012. This is arrant nonsense. Private equity firms like Bain Capital measure their investment performance in terms of their "annualized internal rate of return." This is the number most frequently cited to investors. That measure gives the highest rating to the fastest deals. Hence the claim that the Experian deal, which trebled investors' money, produced an "implied gross annualized internal rate of return of 6,636%," just because it was fast.

In private equity, short-term profits are the best profits.

Romney gave an interesting insight into his perspective when he gave an interview to the Associated Press interview way back in September, 2005. He was explaining how his years of experience in business had taught him how to lead.

To get things done in the private sector, he said, "You have to get consensus of the group." Most businesspeople would agree. But what did he mean by "the group?" "You have to get the shareholders to agree, and the bankers to agree, the board to agree, the other members of management to agree," he said.

There is no mention of the customer. There is no mention of the production staff, salesmen, suppliers, or local communities. Even the managers are only ranked fourth on his list, after all the money folks. Main Street, meet Wall Street. Ask someone who runs a restaurant or a small business – or even a medium-sized business – if this is how he or she thinks. Ask them if their top three concerns are "the shareholders…the bankers…and the board." Even businessmen who run really big companies – from Exxon to Microsoft – don't think like this. Do you think Steve Jobs at Apple spent his time thinking about "the bankers"?

Herman Cain nailed it. The former pizza company executive crashed and burned as a presidential candidate, but he knew something about business. When the Republican candidates met in Las Vegas for a CNN debate in October, 2011, he treated Romney politely but firmly.

"There's one difference between the two of us in terms of our experience," Cain said. "With all due respect, his business experience has been more Wall Street-oriented, mine has been more Main Street. I have managed small companies. I've actually had to clean the parking lot."

Mitt Romney and Bain Capital owned Domino's Pizza. But do you think Romney ever swept the parking lot?

4

OTHER PEOPLE'S MONEY

Our image of a self-made man is someone like Benjamin Franklin, who was born to a candle-maker in Boston and couldn't afford to finish school. Or Andrew Carnegie, who arrived on the boat from Scotland at age thirteen with barely a cent to his name and worked his way up to become one of the richest men in the world. These are American icons: People who came from humble backgrounds, and pulled themselves up by their bootstraps.

Mitt Romney has sometimes felt the urge to try to cast himself in a similar light. "I went off on my own," he said during the CNN debate in South Carolina in January, 2012. "I didn't inherit money from my parents. What I have, I earned. I worked hard, the American way." In response to a remark from Newt Gingrich, he replied, "[Mr.] Speaker, you've indicated that somehow I didn't earn that money. I have earned the money that I have. I didn't inherit it."

Mitt Romney is worth at least $250 million – and probably had plenty more before setting up trusts for his heirs. If elected, he would be one of the richest men ever to serve in the White House.

We have all heard stories about Romney's wealth. We have heard about the elevator he is building for his cars in his California beach house. We have heard about his wife's "pair of Cadillacs." In a televised debate in 2011 he offered Rick Perry a $10,000 bet. I have to confess I have a different reaction to these things from a lot of people. Okay, so I think Romney is very foolish to flaunt his wealth in some of these cases. (If you are running for president, the new car elevator in La Jolla can wait.) But I don't really care. If I had a house on Lake Winnipesaukee, in New Hampshire, I'd probably jetski there too, as Romney did during the summer of 2012. And I quite liked his bet against Rick Perry. I thought it showed some moxie.

Mitt Romney has suggested that any criticism or scrutiny is motivated by envy or class warfare. "I know the Democrats want to go after the fact that I've been successful," he said during the debate in South Carolina in January, 2012. "I'm not going to apologize for being successful."

Most Americans respect people who have made their money, especially if they can respect how it was made. Furthermore, most voters would probably welcome more self-made businessmen and businesswomen in politics. Such people may have something to offer. Many public servants are otherwise unemployable.

Voters are nonetheless entitled to ask questions about Romney's wealth, and about how he made it. Why? First, because Mitt Romney has made it an issue himself. He has frequently equated wealth with "success," and he has tried to imply that he made it all himself, the hard way. Second, how he made it reflects on his credentials for the White House. One of his main campaign arguments has centered on his apparent business success. If Romney had emerged from Bain Capital with a $1 million IRA and driving a second-hand Nissan, his campaign would look very different. And third, how Mitt Romney made his money also says a lot that is important about public policy, and how our system works today. It's material.

So how did Mitt Romney really come by his spectacular fortune? How far is he really a self-made man?

His father, George Romney, made his money in the 1950s while he was running American Motors. Mitt was just a child at the time. Romney, Sr. was asked by the board to take over when the CEO died. The stock collapsed. Banks were threatening to call in their loans. George Romney believed in the company so much that he took all the money he had saved to buy the family a bigger house and plunged it into AMC stock instead.

Then he set out to save the company.

In the years that followed, AMC survived, then prospered. It pioneered fuel-efficient cars like the Rambler. The stock, as mentioned earlier, went from $6 to $96. George Romney and his family were rich.

The family moved to the exclusive Detroit suburb of Bloomfield Hills when Mitt was six years old. He was sent to an elite private school nearby. Later, in his first year of college at Stanford, his allowance was so generous that he was able to sneak home from San Francisco to Detroit on many weekends to see his girlfriend Ann Davies (now his wife). How much did that cost? According to Kayak.com a roundtrip ticket between San Francisco and Detroit today will cost you about $500. It was probably about the same in real terms back then.

As a young man, Romney had opportunities and connections few people his age could dream of. When he got married at 22, the President sent his congratulations. A future president, Gerald Ford, was among the guests.

Romney went to Harvard for a four-year graduate degree in 1971. He took along two valuable financial assets, courtesy of his father.

The first was a big pile of stock. "The stock came from Mitt's father," Ann Romney told the Boston Globe in 1994. "When he took over American Motors, the stock was worth nothing. But he invested Mitt's birthday money year to year...Five years later, stock that had been $6 a share was $96 and Mitt cashed it so we could live and pay for education."

How much did he have? We don't know for sure, but Ann Romney has said George had invested at least "a few thousand" on Mitt's behalf. If that is colloquial for, say, $5,000 to $10,000, it would have meant that by 1971 Mitt Romney may have had anywhere from $50,000 to $150,000. In today's money, that would be between $280,000 and $850,000. Not bad for a young graduate student.

The second asset was a $5,000 "loan" that George Romney made to Mitt and Ann so that they could avoid run-down rental accommodation in Cambridge and buy a $42,000 house in Belmont, an upscale suburb where they still live. The value of that loan is about $28,000 in today's money, and the house about $235,000.

It was privilege enough to be at Harvard forty years ago. But few others in the class could afford to escape the rent trap and buy into Boston's exclusive real estate market, or to live on stock from their father.

When Mitt Romney ran for the United States Senate in 1994, Ann gave an interview with the Boston Globe's Jack Thomas. "We were living on the edge," she said of those early years. She had been home with the children; Mitt was studying. "Neither one of us had a job, because Mitt had enough of an investment from stock that we could sell off a little at a time...We had no income except the stock we were chipping away at."

Margery Eagan, my colleague at the Boston Herald, couldn't resist. "I realized at that moment that Ann Romney has not a clue about my life, nor the lives of anybody I know," she wrote in her column a few days later.

Ann Romney, she added, "lives in Belmont, only a 20-minute ride from downtown. It may as well be Mars."

Mitt Romney graduated in 1975 and got his first full-time job at the age of 28. George Romney lived for another twenty years, until 1995. By the time he died, Mitt Romney was 48 and already a very rich man. So the money that he would have received from his father's estate went to Mormon charities instead. It allowed him to claim, "I didn't inherit it." This is semantics.

There is absolutely nothing wrong with growing up wealthy. There is nothing wrong with getting a great start in life, or in having parents who can afford to send you to the best schools. But there is something ominous about denying it – especially if it means you don't realize just how lucky you were.

As Romney said to Texas governor Rick Perry during a primary debate in Tampa, Florida in September, 2011, "If you're dealt four aces, that doesn't make you necessarily a great poker player." Romney's been dealt numerous aces in his life. Why can't he admit it?

The denial doesn't stop there, either.

In the Republican debate in South Carolina in January, 2012 Mitt Romney also bragged that his financial success was entirely without any government help whatsoever. "I was in business 25 years," he said. "I don't recall a single day saying, oh, thank heavens Washington is there for me. Thank heavens. I said, please get out of my way, let me start a business and put Americans to work."

Really? Let's look at the record.

The government's pension support system had to put in $44 million to support workers' pensions at GS Steel after Bain Capital left town, as Reuters reported. When Mitt Romney went back to Bain & Co., his old strategy consultants, in 1991 to rescue it from bankruptcy, the Federal Deposit Insurance Corporation wrote off a $10 million Bain debt. The FDIC is backed by the federal government. It was set up during the New Deal to protect mom and pop savers from the collapse of their local bank. Whether the FDIC should be forgiving debts owed by feckless millionaires and management consultants is a subject for debate. Were these the only two instances in which federal bodies ended up picking up the tab for a Romney-related business? We may never know for sure.

There is a broader sense in which Bain Capital, like any American business, has benefited from the actions of the federal government. Anyone who's taken civics in school knows the basics – the government paves the roads, educates the workers, upholds the laws of contract, maintains sound financial markets and so on.

We've seen how Mitt Romney and Bain Capital made their money, by taking bets on companies with borrowed money. Some of those deals went sour, either for the bankers, the bondholders, the employees, or all of them. In some cases, creditors lost a lot of money, even while Bain Capital made money. In the language of Main Street, the company welched on its debts. If Romney thinks the U.S. government played no role in allowing that to happen, he should try running a business the same way in, oh, let's say…Sicily.

OPM

Mitt Romney likes to tell the story about his dad at American Motors. Americans everywhere warm to the story. George Romney risked everything he had on his dream. He took a big gamble, and to those who take the risk should go the rewards. That's how it works for people who run small businesses as well as big ones. The dry-cleaner, the couple who owns a restaurant, the person who makes a new invention in his garage and takes out a mortgage to start his company: This is the American way.

It has almost nothing to do with how Mitt Romney made his money.

Yes, Mitt invested some of his own money alongside his investors in the Bain Capital funds. But that was only part of the story. Where he really made his fortune was from the technique known on Wall Street as OPM: Other People's Money.

Mitt Romney got a free ride. Bain Capital risked its clients' money, and the money of bondholders, on investments. When those investments boomed during the bull market, the people at Bain Capital – and especially Mitt Romney, the CEO – took an enormous slice of the upside.

How? For starters, they charged the clients 1.5% to 2% in base fees just for running the fund. Then they collected at least 20% of the funds' returns, or profits, as a "performance fee." Most of that came in the form of free stock in the fund.

Mitt Romney, reported Kranish and Helman, personally collected between 5% and 10% of Bain Capital's entire cut, at least on some deals.

The fees were even higher than they seemed. Private equity funds don't charge that 1.5% or 2% money management fee on the money they are actually managing. They charge it on the money that the investors have promised to commit to the fund, even before the managers get around to finding the right investments. In reality, managers usually only end up investing half of all the money committed. Yet they charge the fee on all of it. "On average, [only] half of the capital committed to a private equity fund is actually invested," wrote Oxford's Phalippou in the Journal of Economic Perspectives in 2007. "Hence a 2 percent fee on capital committed is the same as a 4 percent fee on capital invested." When I spoke to Phalippou, he said that the typical private equity firm ends up charging clients about 7% of their assets per year, in management fees, "portfolio costs," and so on.

As for the 20% or 30% "performance fee," Bain Capital insiders like Romney created yet another way to make money out of other people's money. As the Wall Street Journal reported, they were entitled to a special class of stock in their funds that was not available to clients. That special class, known as the "A" class, paid out even bigger returns when investments went well.

Normally if you want higher returns, you have to take higher risk. If you or your grandmother wanted the equivalent of Bain Capital's "A" shares, you – or your grandma – would have to go out and buy derivatives known as "stock options," which gain a lot of value if an investment does very well. Those options are expensive to ordinary people. You pay a big premium for the lottery ticket. And they expire quickly, usually within a year or two.

Bain Capital's "A" stock? Not so much. The Bain Capital managers got them as a privilege of working there.

If the market had done badly, these "A" class stocks would have been a dud. They wouldn't have made any money. But in a gigantic boom, like the one in the eighties and nineties, they were better than gold.

As we've already seen, Bain Capital's investors were getting a ride on the backs of the bondholders (and sometimes the employees) thanks to the bankruptcy code. Meanwhile Romney was getting an easy ride on the back of his investors. Someone else thought up the business, other people took the risks, and his entire team sweated bullets to run the company, including the nine months when he was away running for the Senate. But as late as the mid-1990s, as he later revealed in *Turnaround*, he had still kept 100% of the voting stock. That got him the lion's share of the money. No wonder he didn't want to stand down as CEO – even after moving to Salt Lake City to run the Olympics.

There is nothing illegal or immoral about this. But it is a stretch to claim that this is out of the Ben Franklin school of self-help.

Uncle Sam's Money

If you earn $1 million next year – lucky you – then you will need to pay a lot of tax. You will need to pay income tax at 35% on everything above a few hundred thousand dollars. You will need to pay state taxes, and maybe a city tax as well. You will have to pay Social Security taxes on your first $100,000 or so of income, and Medicare taxes on everything. In total you could end up in some cases paying much more than $400,000 in total taxes.

Wouldn't it be great if you didn't have to? Wouldn't it be terrific if you got to pay much lower taxes – or even none at all? And wouldn't it be even better if you could defer any taxes you did need to pay for as long as you liked?

You might dream, but for Mitt Romney and others in private equity this is a reality. Thanks to the U.S. tax code, they get a privilege that you don't.

When they start their private equity funds, they get valuable free stock in the fund as compensation. But the IRS doesn't treat that as taxable income. The IRS just ignores it. The partners don't have to pay any tax on the money at that time.

And when they come to cash in the stock, the IRS does them a second favor. Even though the money was payment for their services, it is not counted as taxable income. Instead it is counted as capital gains, and is taxed at a lower rate. Today the rate is just 15%, even for billionaires.

This is called the "carried interest" rule. It has saved Mitt Romney tens of millions of dollars.

Members of Congress know this is unfair. They admitted as much back in the 1990s, when they specifically restricted this kind of free ride...for everyone except private equity and hedge fund managers. Corporate executives used to get similar breaks on their incentive stock options, but Congress passed a law in the 1990s to cap that because it was being so widely abused. The free ride for private equity managers continues. It has been embraced, or accepted, by both parties.

"A partnership profits interest is the single most tax-efficient form of compensation available without limitation to highly paid executives," wrote Victor Fleischer, a law professor at the University of Illinois, in a 2008 paper in the NYU Law Review.

This break is especially valuable in a rising market, because it allows private equity managers to make big bets for free. It lets them gamble with Uncle Sam's money.

How? They get to bet on their own funds with pretax dollars. If the fund does badly, only the IRS loses. The private equity managers owe nothing. But if the market booms and the fund rises, the private equity managers – not the IRS – get most of the profits. These are basically free chips at the casino, thanks to other taxpayers.

Bain Capital's tax breaks went further. As the Wall Street Journal revealed, Bain Capital had a special IRA which allowed insiders to shelter another $30,000 of their income, far more than what is available to most workers, and they were able to use those IRAs to hold the high-volatility "A" stock in their funds. The net result was spectacular profits, with outside investors, bondholders and Uncle Sam effectively providing most of the capital, and taking the risk.

Bottom line? Mitt Romney made his money thanks to an incredibly lucky start in life, the protections of the bankruptcy code, the clever use of other people's money, and tax breaks. Maybe there's nothing wrong with these things. But they are relevant.

The Bain Connection

Mitt Romney left Bain Capital in 1999 or 2002, depending on how you look at it. But you never really leave. His statement of personal financial disclosures and his 2010 tax return show that he still has much of his wealth tied up in Bain Capital funds. And he remains close to private equity, and the world of finance, in other important ways.

In 2008, Barack Obama outraised John McCain on Wall Street by $16 million to $9 million. Many liberals were surprised that President Obama didn't go after the Wall Street banks more aggressively after the financial crisis. They shouldn't have been.

This time around, it's a different picture. Through March 31, 2012, President Obama had raised less than $3 million from Wall Street. Mitt Romney, before he had even clinched the Republican nomination, had raised more than $8 million.

It doesn't end there.

Mitt Romney's key ally in his 2012 election victory was the "independent" Super PAC, Restore Our Future. By the time the primaries were over it had spent $45 million helping him to victory – $40 million of it on negative advertising against his opponents.

Where did Restore Our Future get all that money? According to documents filed with the Federal Election Committee, and analyzed by the Center for Responsive Politics in Washington, the biggest contributors included a lot of Wall Street.

Hedge fund managers John Paulson (Paulson & Co.), Julian Robertson (Tiger Management), Paul Singer (Elliott Associates), Ken Griffin (Citadel), and Robert Mercer (Renaissance) gave $1 million apiece. Others came through with $100,000, $200,000, or whatever they had lying around. Two managers at Blackstone Group gave $100,000 apiece. Managers at Bain Capital gave $2 million. Steven Webster at

Avista Capital Partners, another private equity company, gave $1 million. Henry Kravis and others at KKR, yet another private equity company, gave $275,000.

Maybe they like Mitt Romney because he's a swell guy. He talks their language because he is one of them. He didn't make his money in manufacturing or services. He made his money in private equity. He knows these people. Many of them invested in Bain Capital funds. Many are Harvard business or law school alumni. Romney's election would continue the growing dominance of finance in the U.S. economy, a dominance only briefly interrupted by the 2008-9 crisis.

There again, maybe they like him because he promises to repeal the regulations imposed on Wall Street in the wake of the past two crises. The Sarbanes-Oxley regulations were passed in 2002 following scandals at Enron, WorldCom and other companies. The Dodd-Frank law was passed in 2010 in reaction to the 2008 financial crash. Romney has promised to repeal them both, though he says he will bring in newer, smarter laws instead.

There's another possibility. Wall Street may like Romney because his tax plans should save them a lot of dollars. Most of these people still make their money from capital gains. Romney wants to keep those taxes low. What would he do about the carried interest loophole? It's an open question.

Cynics may say: Follow the money. We'll see.

5

THE CONSULTANT

MANAGER: I'd like to go ahead and welcome a new member of our team. This is Bob Slydell. Bob is a 'consultant.' He's going to be, sort-of, uh, helping us out a little here, asking some questions, maybe seeing if there are some ways we can make things run a little more smoothly around here.

EMPLOYEE (UNDER HIS BREATH): We are so screwed.

"Office Space" (1999)

The late 1990s movie Office Space has a cult following. It features a bored Silicon Valley software engineer, Peter Gibbons, who decides to rip off his company. What makes the movie so popular is its brutal and pin-sharp take on corporate life – from "Hawaiian shirt day," to receptionists with shrieking voices, to petty-minded bosses obsessed with paperwork. Everyone who has worked in a modern office knows what this is like.

Early in the movie, the company brings in two management consultants – both named "Bob" – to cut costs. The managers claim the arrival of "the Bobs" is completely innocuous, but the employees know better.

Eventually the Bobs tell Gibbons that they are going to fire his two best friends:

GIBBONS: You're going to fire Samir and Michael?
BOB PORTER: Oh, yeah, we're going to bring in some entry-level graduates, farm some work out to Singapore. It's the usual deal.
BOB SLYDELL: It's standard operating procedure.

As Gibbons leaves, he says with mock cheer, "Good luck with your layoffs, all right? I hope your firings go really well!"

Office Space should be required viewing for anyone who wants to understand Mitt Romney – the candidate, or the public official. The media usually refers to Romney as a "businessman," or a "CEO," or a "venture capital guy," but that's not really precise. Romney didn't start out as an entrepreneur joining a risky new venture. He didn't set up a company in a garage. He didn't even work his way up a big multinational like General Motors or Procter & Gamble.

Romney was a strategy consultant, right from the start. He didn't run companies. He didn't make decisions. He just gave advice to the CEO. As he said later in *Turnaround,* he didn't run companies and he had no actual experience of project management.

Romney, in short, was a "Bob."

This explains a great deal about the way he operates, the way he governed in Massachusetts, and the way he has campaigned.

He trained at the finishing school for consultants, Harvard, where he earned joint degrees in business administration and law. Then he went to the Boston Consulting Group, followed by Bain & Co. Both companies are famous blue-chip "Bob" firms. Making money in private equity, running the Salt Lake City Olympics, being governor of Massachusetts: Those things came much later. Romney was a consultant, or training to be one, from the age of twenty-four to thirty-seven. These are key years. They are when we typically form our opinions as adults. They are when we build the foundations of our careers and our skill sets. What we do in our twenties and thirties typically sets us up for life.

Romney was a very successful consultant. He was seen as the rising star of Bain, and a potential successor to the founder in due course. If you want to understand Romney, you have to understand management consultants. They have three stand-out characteristics:

Rule #1: Consultants are all about the details

"My favorite thing to do is to bathe in data," Romney told Matthew Rees at the American Enterprise Institute in a 2006 interview. Or, as he wrote in *Turnaround*, "My ten years in consulting and my sixteen years in venture capital and private equity taught me that there are answers in numbers." There was, he added, "gold in numbers. Pile the budgets on my desk and let me wallow. Numbers can help solve a mystery. I discover trends, form hypotheses, most of which fail but lead to others that are more fruitful. Almost without exception, I learn something that is key to the success of the enterprise."

There speaks a "Bob."

Most management consultants like getting down into the minutiae. They don't do the vision thing. It's their role to crunch the numbers, build spreadsheets, and analyze products, markets and operations.

Management consultants tend to be incrementalists. They tend to be pragmatic problem solvers. They are very good at taking the work or vision of others and making it a little better. They don't tend to be the guys who take the big leaps.

Mitt Romney has always struggled to offer a vision. On the campaign trail he's taken to reciting the words to America the Beautiful. Or he says stuff like this: "The Republican Party is a party of the future and with a vision. Ronald Reagan had a vision for where he was going to take America. We have to once again take people forward. And that vision is the new frontier of the 21st century." That's what he said during a debate in June, 2007.

Now contrast that with how he sounds when he's allowed to get down into the details. Here he is, for example, writing about global warming and fuel efficiency in *No Apology*: "McKinsey & Company conducted a study in 2009 to determine how much the emission of global greenhouse gases could be reduced worldwide and at what cost…They evaluated the abatement potential and the costs for more than two hundred different abatement opportunities. On page 238 is a bar chart illustrating the summary findings…"

Which one is the real Mitt Romney? What do you think?

Michael Kranish and Scott Helman in *The Real Romney* reported that in preparing for the Iowa caucuses in 2007, Romney became fascinated with the idea of "micro-targeting" voters – another word for incredibly detail-oriented customer segmentation. In micro-targeting, you find out everything about each voter and then send them messages targeted specifically around their individual preferences. ("Dear Mrs Jones, As a cat-loving, stamp-collecting Baptist you're probably wondering where the main presidential candidates stand on the issues that matter to you…") It's a classic technique for a consultant. Romney and his team took it to extremes. "We had a lot of data but no information," complained Douglas Gross, his Iowa chairman. While Romney was getting lost in the little details, the candidate wasn't building an actual narrative or a coalition behind his candidacy. Mike Huckabee, who would win Iowa, didn't waste money on "micro-targeting."

Consultants, like "the Bobs" in Office Space, are most famous for laying people off. Often senior management will hire consultants just so they can blame them for the round of layoffs that the company already knows it needs. The main reason consultants cut costs so often isn't because they are mean or sociopaths, but because it's something they understand. It's something they can easily recommend to almost any client, and that is likely to lead to higher profits. It doesn't require creativity or vision, merely analytical skills. Consultants, for example, will go into a chemical plant that is running at a loss and compare its costs to those of its main competitors. They may work out that it employs 10% more people and uses 15% more raw materials than the most profitable plants. They will then tell the company how to bring those costs down in line with the competition.

Or they will go into an office of thirty people and work out how they can do the same amount of work with only twenty-five. If you are wondering why you are working longer hours these days, you can thank a consultant. Thank "the Bobs."

Mitt Romney's main achievements in public life have been consulting projects. They've been about managing details and cutting costs.

The day after he was elected governor of Massachusetts, according to the American Enterprise Institute's profile in 2006, Romney "convened a meeting of senior advisers to talk about restructuring, with an emphasis on overhauling the way Cabinet departments would report to him." He brought in his former employers, Bain and the Boston Consulting Group, to find ways to cut costs, and to restructure higher education, and health and human services.

Romney faced an immediate budget crunch. As noted earlier, it would turn out to be about $1.2 billion, around 5% of state revenues. It was a problem made for a Bain consultant. "I went through every single cut with every single one of the executive offices and the Cabinet-level agencies," he told the Globe with satisfaction a couple of months later. "It's a process I am used to. It's the same thing which we did at the Olympics. It's the same thing we did at the consulting firm."

Standard operating procedure. The only thing missing was farming some work out to Singapore (and Hawaiian shirt day).

Even Romney's signature achievement, the universal healthcare law now known as "RomneyCare," began this way.

The state was grappling with skyrocketing medical bills. It was picking up the tab for treating all those citizens who had no health insurance and no money. The so-called "uncompensated care pool" was in crisis. If the state didn't find a solution, it risked losing federal Medicaid funds.

Romney brought in Deloitte & Touche, consultants, to work out what to do.

It was a classic consultants' job. As writer Matthew Rees put it: "Romney had started, naturally, with a Bain-style strategic audit, pulling together experts from business, academia, and government, and posing a few basic – though frequently overlooked – questions: Who exactly was uninsured? Why were they uninsured? What could be done to enable people to keep their health coverage even if they switched jobs or worked as independent contractors?"

They surveyed 5,000 households and crunched the numbers. They found that most of the uninsured fell into two categories: Those who could afford insurance but didn't buy it, and those who just couldn't afford it.

RomneyCare was a non-ideological way of dealing with both problems. The former were told to stop free-riding: The state required them to buy insurance or pay an annual "fine" into the pot. The latter were offered subsidized insurance.

Sensible. Pragmatic. A solution you could recommend to any CEO.

Robert Moffit, a healthcare expert at the conservative Heritage Foundation, told the AEI that when he went to brief Romney on the issues he was surprised to find the governor briefing him about details instead.

It has been a similar story throughout Mitt Romney's career. In 1991 Bill Bain asked him to come back to Bain & Co. as emergency CEO to rescue it from potential bankruptcy.

It was a details job, not a vision one. Romney thrived. He canceled rent checks and pressured lenders to accept losses. He even got the Federal Deposit Insurance Corporation, the agency of the federal government that guarantees your bank deposits, to accept a $10 million loss on some loans.

Now consider one of Romney's most dramatic success stories, what he calls his "turnaround" at the Salt Lake City Olympics. When Romney took over the Games in 1999, the previous management had just been fired in an alleged scandal. Romney said in *Turnaround* that the Games faced a budget shortfall of $379 million in a total budget of $1.9 billion.

In the years since, he has often presented this as a dramatic rescue, a miracle of executive leadership. If he hadn't stepped in, he told the Boston Globe in March, 2002, "We wouldn't have had an Olympics in Salt Lake City in 2002."

Really? The scandal was "troublesome," Mike Moran, a spokesman for the U.S. Olympic Committee, told the Boston Globe in 2002, "but the Games were never in jeopardy. The Games were never in danger of being moved. Ever." Robert Garff, a member of the organizing committee, added that "yes, we were out of balance, but we had [three] years to organize that. In my mind, there was no sense of panic." And Ken Bullock, executive director of the Utah League of Cities and Towns, and a member of the Olympic organizing committee, said dryly of Romney: "He deserves credit, just not as much as he thinks he does."

The scandal wasn't anything to do with preparation for the games anyway. It was just about gifts allegedly given to the International Olympic Committee to help win the bid.

Romney's key acts were to steady the ship and to cut the budget by more than $100 million. He quickly introduced austerity measures. Romney gloried in newspaper accounts of his tough new regime. When a local paper published a cartoon that showed him standing in front of "MittFrugal's," he had it framed.

One of his first austerity moves was to start charging $1 a slice for the pizzas being served on site to all those working on the Olympics, including the volunteers. It was a symbolic move, a good-looking bullet point on the presentation to management. How much difference did it make in a $1.9 billion budget? Not much. The entire population of Salt Lake county was less than a million. How much pizza could they eat?

Romney remains the consultant at heart. In the fall of 2011 he unveiled a 59-point plan for the economy. He couldn't understand why it didn't set his campaign alight.

Rule #2: Consultants don't like risks

The final days of July, 2011, were hair-raising ones for the country and the world. As financial markets reeled, Democrats and Republicans in Washington took hard-line negotiations over the federal budget right down to the wire.

With days to go to raise the ceiling on the national debt, Democrats wouldn't agree on spending cuts. The Republicans wouldn't agree on tax hikes. The two sides came close to triggering a U.S. debt crisis. Stock markets slumped. Gold soared. In the aftermath Standard & Poor's cut America's bond rating.

Shouldn't this have been Mitt Romney's moment? Shouldn't this have been the point where he stepped up, took on leadership, and showed both sides a way to resolve the problem?

The crisis was tailor-made for the skills Romney says he will bring to government.

Here, after all, is a candidate who talks a lot about his financial background and expertise; someone who is used to cutting costs, crunching numbers, and finding solutions; someone, furthermore, who claims to be above partisanship, and who says he is willing to work with people on both sides of the aisle to get things done.

Down in Washington, both the Democratic president and the Republican Congress were retreating to their ideological bunkers and putting the economy in peril.

Where was Mitt? He retreated into his entourage and wouldn't take a position. "When he faced questions at his campaign stops," reported the Associated Press, "he said he wasn't privy to the behind-the-scenes negotiations, and his campaign aides refused to elaborate on his thinking about the proposals in serious play."

That answer made little logical sense. You do not need to be privy to negotiations to be able to offer proposals or an analysis. The crisis called out for a big speech.

Later, during a debate in February, 2012, Romney said he wanted a debt ceiling deal "only if we [had] a cut, cap, and balance provision put in place." This was no answer at all. Saying you want to balance the budget through "cut, cap, and balance" is like saying you plan to diet by "losing weight." Clearly if the federal government is going to close a $1 trillion deficit, some things will need to be cut, some things will need to be capped, and in the end you want to achieve balance.

So speaks the consultant.

Outsiders often find this confusing. How can Romney be a successful businessman and yet be so timid? How can you make a fortune without taking big, bold bets?

Great leaders take great risks.

All the great men and women of the past put their necks on the line. All of those who have achieved great things did so by taking a gamble. The pilgrims risked everything when they set sail on the Mayflower. Abraham Lincoln wagered everything on the war. Harry Truman took an enormous gamble when he fired Douglas MacArthur. When we think of leaders in the world of business, we think of people who took risks too, such as Andrew Carnegie or Henry Ford.

Even your average entrepreneur – from a contractor to a restaurant owner – knows about big risks. They remortgage the house to start their business. They invest in a new factory when the economy is in a slump. They launch a new product line that might not work out.

Not so with strategy consultants. They make recommendations, but they don't own the results. They don't take the risks. The client does.

When Romney was first asked in December, 2006 whether he supported a possible troop "surge" in Iraq, his initial response – according to the Associated Press – was "I'm not going to weigh in. I'm still a governor." He quickly changed course, and began backing President Bush. However, John McCain successfully hammered him for his initial equivocation during the debates a year later.

Asked during a CNN debate in New Hampshire in June, 2011 what he would do in Afghanistan, Romney said he would only bring home troops "based upon the conditions on the ground determined by the generals."

That earned him an instant Harry Truman smack-down

from Ron Paul. "I wouldn't wait for my generals," retorted the feisty Texas congressman. In that scenario, he said, "I'm the commander in chief. I make the decisions. I tell the generals what to do."

Maybe Romney's aversion to risk explains why, in 2008, he waited until it was too late to make a speech about his religion, and why he's been willing to trim his sails, time and time again, to the prevailing winds – on abortion, on gay rights, on global warming.

Romney's equivocations exasperate his fans and infuriate his opponents. But none of them should be surprised. If you want to understand the man, go back almost 40 years.

Mitt Romney graduated from Harvard Business and Law Schools at an exciting time. It was the mid-seventies. New technologies like video, wireless, and personal computing were just emerging. Bill Gates was setting up Microsoft. Steve Jobs and Steve Wozniak were setting up Apple. It was the birth of a new age.

The greater Boston area, where Romney was based, was right in the thick of things. It was the home of booming high-tech companies like Digital Equipment, Polaroid, and Wang Laboratories. Massachusetts, largely thanks to the presence of colleges like the Massachusetts Institute of Technology, was a thriving high tech hub. A business graduate in his twenties looking for adventure and a chance for entrepreneurship had plenty of choices.

It says a lot about Mitt Romney that in this environment he nonetheless chose what was, and remains, the ultimate "safe" choice for a business school graduate. Consulting is a low-risk job for those starting out. The starting salaries are very good. The big firms are stable and highly profitable. They weather recessions well. Young consultants get a broad exposure to different industries very quickly. They gain skills and experience that will look good on their resumes later on.

Consulting, bluntly, is a bit boring. (Trust me. I know.)

Romney himself in *No Apology* tells the story of how, some years later, he was back at business school recruiting on behalf of Bain. He offered a job to the young Steve Ballmer, who turned him down in favor of a young, high-risk technology company – Microsoft. Today Ballmer is the CEO. Without any sense of self-awareness, Romney recounts his surprise at the young Ballmer's choice.

Ballmer, he wrote, "confessed that he was leaning toward turning us down in favor of joining a start-up business with a friend from college. I pointed out that if he did, he'd make far less money and be committed to a tiny company that could easily fail. But, in the end, he rejected the bird in the hand we offered him in favor of birds in the bush."

Twenty-five years later, Ballmer reminded him of the incident. They were meeting in Bill Gates' house. By then Ballmer was worth $15 billion.

Then consider the story of how Romney got his start in Bain Capital, the company that would make him rich (by most standards, if not by the standards of Ballmer and Gates). Today he likes to present it as a bold risk, a gamble. He was an "entrepreneur" who saw the future and started a company. The truth, as reported in numerous accounts, was very different.

In 1983 Mitt Romney was a consultant at Bain & Co., building relationships with the clients, playing the game. And by all accounts he was very good at it.

One day his boss called. The company's founder and CEO, Bill Bain, had an idea. He had watched as Bain & Co. had helped clients generate greater profits. Now, he decided, he wanted a piece of the action too. He thought Bain should start investing in companies itself and then use the same techniques to boost their bottom lines; that way, he reasoned, the firm would reap the full rewards of its expertise. His dream, in short, was to start a private equity firm. It would take advantage of Bain's enormous infrastructure of client contacts, industry expertise, consultants and business partners.

Bain said he needed a good, tough young manager to take the lead – someone old enough and mature enough to handle the responsibility, but still young and hungry enough to take a risk.

Mitt Romney, then 36 and a young partner, was right in the sweet spot. And he had struck a real chord with Bill Bain. The older man saw him as a protégé.

The offer was a golden opportunity for Romney. Take a gamble. Start a new business, with powerful backers behind him.

However, as the Boston Globe later revealed, Romney's initial response was to pass. The new venture just sounded too risky, he told Bain. It was too much of a gamble. What if it went wrong? What if the investments didn't make as much money as he hoped? He said he was happy with his safer consulting job. He was content to go along as he had been, dealing with clients, attending meetings, collecting his big bonuses.

Your typical entrepreneur overcomes resistance from people around him to pursue his dream. Romney? He was the anti-entrepreneur. His own boss was offering to set up a company for him and give him the big chair – and Romney was turning him down.

Bain was stunned. He offered to sweeten the pot. Okay, he told Romney: What if I take away all the risk? I'll give you a no-lose, sweetheart deal. Start this company for me, and if it goes south, I'll give you your old job back. I'll even give you the bonuses and raises you missed. Romney passed again. What about my reputation, he said. Sure, I'll get my old job back. But people will still say I failed. So Bain added yet more sugar to the pot. If Bain Capital doesn't succeed, he said, I'll cover for you. You'll get your old job back, plus all the bonuses and raises you missed, and I'll tell everyone that I asked you back because we needed you.

The deal was as safe as he could make it. As Bain put it later, "there was no professional or financial risk." It was a free bet.

At last, Mitt Romney agreed.

Bill Bain came up with the idea of Bain Capital. He and his partners and friends put up the money. They footed the bill for the firm's new offices. The Bain network provided access to the deals, financing and industry expertise. All Mitt Romney had to do was turn up for work at his new job and turn left when he came out of the elevator instead of right. He had a no-cut, no-lose deal.

Maybe this was shrewd. Maybe this was a master class in how to play office politics. It is hard, however, to call it risk-taking and "entrepreneurship." Romney wasn't even playing hardball so he would get more of the profits if things went well. He was playing to cover his downside if things went badly. He was covering his rear.

Now consider Romney's election campaigns.

He certainly took a gamble in his first campaign, launching his 1994 losing race against Ted Kennedy. Yet it wasn't as much of a long-shot as he has since claimed. Kennedy was vulnerable. His drinking and shambolic personal life had taken their tolls, physically and politically. Massachusetts Republicans were enjoying a renaissance under the extremely popular governor William Weld. In September, less than two months before the election, polls put Romney level with Kennedy, or slightly ahead.

Yet in the end, he tried to run a safe campaign. (As a frustrated Rush Limbaugh noted at the time, during the second televised debate Romney had barely disagreed with Kennedy at all during the entire hour.)

In his 2002 race for governor, Romney campaigned largely by avoiding controversy. He promised more money for popular programs and lower taxes. How he would square this circle was never seriously questioned. It was what the clients wanted to hear, and in consulting that usually works. He ran vapid, vanilla commercials. When they didn't work he resorted to the old failsafe, and went negative.

Since 2005, when he first began seriously preparing to run for the White House, Romney has tried to run on the inside, taking the safe path.

Bruce Keough, his New Hampshire campaign chairman, told Michael Kranish and Scott Helman that he had urged the candidate in early 2007 to make his message about the economy. "Romney had responded," they reported, "that it would be premature to settle on that message, saying, as Keough recalled it, 'It is early; who knows what the major issues of the day will be by the time we get to the primaries?'" At the time, the first caucuses and primaries were less than a year away. The economy was already showing signs that there was trouble ahead. Yet Romney, the consultant, didn't want to commit himself.

While Romney's natural game is to be cautious, he has developed on the campaign trail a tedious habit of trying to cover for it with false bravado. He is always telling us how he "won't apologize" for all the tough stances he is taking, even while he is taking no tough stances at all. "I make no apology for the fact that I am pro-life," he told the National Journal in 2010, as he was preparing another run for president on the ticket of an ardently pro-life party. "I won't apologize for being successful," he says, repeatedly – as if anyone is expecting him to. "I make no apology," he thundered in 2010, "for my conviction that America's economic and military leadership is not only good for America but also critical for freedom and peace across the world." Are we to imagine that this is a bold stance for any politician, Republican or Democrat? The statement appears in Romney's book, which was entitled, appropriately enough, *No Apology*.

It rings as phony as a management pep speech. It looks

as tacky as Hawaiian shirt day. Romney's pretense that he is being bold just reminds us that he isn't.

Rule #3: Consultants Don't Talk To Grunts

In Office Space, each employee in turn is required to come to a private meeting with "the Bobs," where he is interviewed about his job, and asked to explain why he should keep it. This is the only time "the Bobs" interact with the staff.

Then the Bobs sit down with the senior managers and tell them who to fire.

When they tell Gibbons that they are going to lay off his friends, he asks if they have been told yet. The Bobs look at him in amazement and start laughing. "No, no," says Bob Slydell. "Of course not!"

Strategy consultants like Mitt Romney don't know much about communicating with ordinary people because they never really have to. From the start of their careers, even fresh out of grad school, they are brought into a company by the CEO and they are answerable only to him. They are part of the "inside" clique at the client headquarters and are privy to information that the ordinary employees are not.

It was what startled me most when I first began working as a consultant. Right from the start, as a kid in his twenties straight out of grad school, I was flying business class and meeting top executives. You're insulated from the rank and file. You meet them when you interview them.

This is the environment in which Mitt Romney worked for the first thirteen years of his career. It is a method of operation that is fundamentally elitist. A twenty-eight-year-old consultant walks into an office, and immediately outranks the fifty-year-old line supervisor who has been there for 25 years. Then the 28-year-old consultant sits down with the sixty-year-old man who started the company and tells him how to run it better.

The process attracts a lot of people who don't really want to get their hands dirty or mix with everyone else. Consultants have a reputation for being stiff, arrogant and aloof.

Romney moves around in an entourage, isolated from voters, the media and the public. His circle jealously guards its privacy and keeps the press at a distance. The candidate holds few press conferences, and has limited availability.

By its definition, this aloofness doesn't get reported very much. It is, after all, hard to report on a negative or to show it on a video clip. The public only gets the occasional glimpse – such as the 2008 YouTube footage of Mitt Romney and Eric Fehrnstrom berating Glen Johnson at the Associated Press.

In his book about the Olympic games, *Turnaround*, Romney approvingly quotes a former president of the Mormon church on how to handle press interviews: "At one point he was gently taken to task for 'not answering the question' he was asked. He smiled and replied, 'You get to ask whatever questions you want. I get to give whatever answers I want. That's the deal.' "

Former Time Magazine reporter Ronald Scott was astonished by the hostility and paranoia he encountered from the Romney inner circle when he approached them about his biography. His conclusion: "It had everything to do with control," he wrote.

Bruce Keough recounts how Romney stayed inside his bubble with Fehrnstrom when he traveled through New Hampshire in the run-up to the 2008 primary. "His preference in traveling between events in New Hampshire was to be alone with Eric in the car," he told Kranish and Helman. Every manager, Keough said, knows that "if you want to know how things are going on the factory floor, go talk to the factory workers." Romney, he said, seemed to have little taste for "management by walking around."

Strategy consultants like Romney have risen through a world of business class lounges and limousines, executive suites and boardroom meetings, secluded from the ordinary people in the office or the factory floor.

Think how different this is from the apprenticeship of the typical politician. Anyone who has spent half a day campaigning in a local election knows how far you have to go outside your comfort zone. You meet all kinds of people, including plenty of people you would prefer not to. You never know what the next voter will be like. You knock on a front door, and a little old lady suspiciously warns she'll call the police. You knock on another and it's your opponent's brother (and he doesn't tell you that until he's wasted ten minutes of your time). You knock on another and you are greeted by the ferocious barking of large dogs and the audible cocking of a shotgun. Even the voters who answer the door and talk to you are a mixed bag. One is a supporter. The next wants to complain about his zoning application. The next wants to grill you about the big UFO cover-up. You do this for a few days and you realize you have to learn the charm and flexibility of a successful used car salesman (And then some. After all, the people who turn up at a used car lot are already looking for a car. A politician is a guy disturbing people at home in the middle of the afternoon to try to sell them a used car they don't want.)

It's no wonder the best politicians tend to be glad-handing extroverts. They're people people.

Consultants go through no such experience.

It was no coincidence that the line that stuck to Romney most was Mike Huckabee's joke in 2008, when he said Romney reminded voters of "the guy who laid them off."

Boston Globe metro columnist Brian McGrory was following Romney during the 2002 gubernatorial campaign when the candidate visited Boston's North End, the Italian neighborhood. He had Rudy Giuliani in tow. It was less than a year after 9/11. In Mike's, a famous local pastry shop, someone offered to buy the two men cannoli. Romney looked awkwardly at his watch and said, "No, thanks, I gotta run." Giuliani stepped up, put his arm around the local's shoulders, and said, "No – let me buy you a cannoli!" The crowd cheered.

When he was governor, Mitt Romney was known in the State House for being distant from the rank and file. Even today he is remembered there, not for being a conservative, but for being aloof. That may account for why he was unable to influence them very much.

One of the inevitable consequences of their experiences is that consultants never develop the ability to communicate to ordinary people in a meaningful way. They are used to having all the power. The successful car salesman has no power, so he has to be really good at communicating with the customer. The management consultant doesn't.

Romney lacks the common touch. He can't communicate. His gaffes are almost pathological. What can you say of a presidential candidate who says that he "isn't concerned about the poor," or "likes firing people," or that "corporations are people, my friend"? These were all actual quotes during his primary campaign in the past year. In their context, they were actually quite innocent. Yet they were a hallmark of someone who has spent his life communicating with his fellow executives behind closed doors.

When Romney took over management of the Salt Lake City Olympics, he says he decided early on that he wanted to build morale among the rank and file, and break down the distinctions with the upper management. How did he do it? In *Turnaround*, he recalls proudly, "I instituted a casual dress policy. We had chambray shirts made up with the [Olympic Committee's] insignia; I wore them religiously, almost every day. To my delight, other senior staffers did too." It's lucky he didn't think of Hawaiian shirts. As for the rank and file? If they joined in, Romney doesn't mention it.

This is not someone who built up his own business by, say, selling photocopiers office to office. This is not a guy who built a chain of restaurants and spent his early days dealing with customers, suppliers, kitchen staff and waiters. He was a consultant, never an executive, never a leader. He communicated in a boardroom with top management, with flip charts, and that's how he operates today.

6

A HECKUVA WAY TO RUN A BUSINESS

Maybe America needs a hands-on, can-do executive to take charge and turn things around. Maybe we need a leader with "real world experience" and crisis management skills. Is Mitt Romney that person?

"I've been chief executive officer four times," Romney reminded voters during a debate in Las Vegas in October, 2011, "once for a start-up and three times for turnarounds." In the debate just before the South Carolina primary he boasted of his broad experience: "I worked in business. I worked in helping turn around the Olympics. I worked in helping lead a state. I believe that kind of background and skill is what is essential to restore the American promise."

On the stump and in interviews he talks frequently about his "crisis" and "leadership" skills, his real-world experience at "turnarounds," his can-do expertise. The president, by contrast, has "no experience" and is "out of his depth." As Romney said during the MSNBC debate in September, 2011, the problem with President Obama was that he "had never worked in the economy...he's just over his head, and right now, he's flailing about."

The story of Romney's executive excellence is one his supporters are happy to talk up, too.

"I'm for Mitt Romney because he's got the proven experience as a manager and as a job creator that America needs right now," said Ohio governor John Kasich in April. "He has proved, time and again, that he excels at turning around difficult situations," agreed Rudy Giuliani in a glowing endorsement, citing Romney's great achievements from business to the Olympics.

How far is this true?

As we're going through Mitt Romney's resume, let's look at the major job he's held most recently. It has been a challenging one. It has given him a chance to showcase all his executive and leadership skills to the full. Since January, 2007, Mitt Romney has been a full-time candidate for president of the United States.

In the modern world, a political campaign is a business. Running for national office tests your ability to build a smooth and efficient organization, to pick the right people, put them in the right positions, give them the right tools, and delegate to them the right tasks. It demands that the candidate listen to the optimal advice, pick the optimal strategy, craft the optimal messages, and build the optimal brand – that he understand who his target "customers" are and how to reach them. It demands that he know his own weaknesses as well as his strengths. It tests, in sum, his ability to lead and execute.

How has Mitt Romney done?

It's too soon to reach a conclusion. We'll find out for sure in November. But he's already held this job for at least five and a half years. He's shown us a lot.

Romney's supporters might argue that the candidate has already proven himself, because he has won the nomination of a major party. However, that's hardly a convincing argument. By definition, every candidate for president can say the same thing, including Barry Goldwater, George McGovern, and the "inexperienced" Barack Obama. Furthermore, just as Mitt Romney would have done while interviewing candidates for Bain or Bain Capital, we need to delve a little deeper. How did Romney win? In what context? And what can we learn about him from the way in which he did it?

Consider, first, the situation he faced when he ran for the nomination in 2008.

The Republican field of candidates that year was extremely weak. Just because John McCain went on to win doesn't mean he was somehow inevitable, or even a strong candidate. He wasn't. How easily we forget: Six months before voting began in Iowa, McCain looked dead in the water. He was running low on cash. He was old. He looked like yesterday's man. A lot of the grassroots didn't trust him. He had broken with them time and again, on big issues like the Bush tax cuts and campaign finance reform. He had alienated the influential Christian right. In the end McCain only won by default. The rest of the field was even weaker than he was. They included far-right cranks like Tom Tancredo, Duncan Hunter, and Sam Brownback, and aging TV star Fred Thompson. The front-runner for most of the race was Rudy Giuliani, but he was simply unviable. The former mayor was a twice-divorced supporter of abortion rights. Gary Bauer, a prominent member of the so-called Christian right, said the Republican party would be committing "political suicide" to nominate a pro-choice candidate. Giuliani and McCain polled dead last in a straw poll of Christian conservatives organized by the Family Research Council in October, 2007.

Steve Roberts, longtime Iowa Republican National Committee member, told the National Journal a few months before the Iowa caucus that the party faithful were left cold by the entire field. "None of the candidates have caught real fire yet," he said. "I think you could well see Republicans not turning out" for the Iowa caucuses, he added, "because they're sort of in this depression. I think it probably is a factor that affects every one of the candidates right now."

Republican voters were so lukewarm about their choices, reported Richard Sammon at Kiplinger's Business Forecast, that as late as September, 2007, only one in three Bush campaign donors had made any contribution to a presidential candidate.

Consider Romney's advantages in this situation. He started with a reputation within the party that could have made him acceptable to all sides. He was neither on the conservative or moderate wings. He had no particular enemies. He had a prominent platform as a governor. Holding office in Massachusetts, if it were played right, should have been a big plus: It showed he could win over moderates and some conservative Democrats. He had, as usual, an enormous war chest, a national organization, and the great luxury of personal wealth. He was not tied to the discredited Bush administration or to the Washington establishment. After January, 2007 he had no day job to go to. He had matchless financial contacts: In one day of fund-raising that month he and his supporters were able to raise $6.5 million in donations – more than twice the entire war-chests of the two front-runners, McCain and Giuliani, put together.

He was able to outspend his rivals by a wide margin. The Boston Globe's Michael Kranish and Scott Helman reported that from February to September, 2007, John McCain ran just five commercials in Iowa, while Rudy Giuliani and Mike Huckabee ran none at all. Romney ran 11,000. Over the course of the entire Republican primary campaign, Mitt Romney's campaign spent $32 million on advertising. According to the Wisconsin Advertising Project, that was greater than the amount spent by all the other candidates put together. He spent three times as much as McCain.

Meanwhile, he was handed a perfect opportunity to run a campaign based on his supposed strength, the economy. The housing market started falling more than a year before the Iowa caucuses. Nine months before voting began, the Federal Reserve, Congress, the media and Wall Street were all panicking about "subprime" mortgages and a potential financial crisis. As Mitt Romney might have said to Rick Perry, he was dealt four aces. Yet he managed to lose the hand.

Over the course of thirteen months, from January, 2007 to February, 2008, Mitt Romney managed to blow a staggering $107 million doing so.

How? He picked the wrong strategy, making a crazy tilt toward social conservatives instead of running down the middle of the party. He picked the wrong people, putting untested neophytes in charge of key roles. His campaign had duplicated organizations, fatally crossed internal lines of communication, confusion and drift. He never gave the organization a clear mission or established a clear brand. While Romney's campaign errors were apparent to any sensible observer four years ago, *The Real Romney* has recently revealed just how badly managed the campaign was on the inside.

Warren Tompkins, Romney's senior adviser in South Carolina in the 2008 campaign, told the authors: "The glaring deficiency in the whole operation was the lack of an overall strategist, no single person that at the end of the day raised his hand and said, 'This is what we are going to do.' Somebody has to run the railroad. The irony of it all is, here's a man who sets up apparatus to make decisions, look at the bottom line, cut to the chase, and the campaign was everything but that."

Where was the experienced real world business guy, the hands-on executive, the "turnaround" CEO? No competent executive in the private sector would try to launch a new product on the national stage with a confused brand. None would dismiss urgent and critical feedback from sales staff on the ground. Yet this is what Romney did, persistently, for over a year.

He chose to bet the farm on an early victory in the Iowa caucuses, gambling that both McCain and Giuliani were weak there and that it offered him a great opportunity to get an early win. Yet neither he, nor his campaign manager, seems to have understood Iowa at all. Beth Myers, the Boston aide he bumped up into national campaign manager, later admitted to the Globe reporters how surprised she was there. "If we had known that there would have been 110,000 caucus goers, with a majority of those being evangelical Christians, I would have thought that would have been a tough situation for Mitt to win," she said.

With all due respect to Ms. Myers, anybody who has picked up a newspaper in the last twenty years knows that the Iowa Republican caucus is dominated by evangelical Christians. Televangelist Pat Robertson came second there as long ago as 1988. But apparently this was news to Mitt Romney – and to the person he picked as his campaign manager. What sort of market research is this?

Romney hired Alex Castellanos, a well-regarded Republican media strategist, to help craft his message. And then he hired Stuart Stevens and Russ Schriefer, another pair of media strategists, to do the same. Romney called this "the Bain Way" and said he wanted creative tension and disagreements. Any businessman rolling out a product in a national campaign in a matter of months would call it a recipe for disaster, and so it proved.

Duplication didn't just take place in media matters. An aide later called it "a Noah's Ark campaign…there were two of everything."

As noted earlier, Romney's New Hampshire campaign

chairman, Bruce Keough, complained that he couldn't get any time to talk to the candidate. When Romney visited New Hampshire, he later said, the candidate preferred to ride around with Fehrnstrom.

Business leaders know that you listen to people on the ground, close to the customers.

Consider how Romney handled an asset that should have been an ace: New Hampshire governor Judd Gregg, one of his national co-chairmen. New Hampshire, home of the first primary, was a vital state for Romney. Few people know its politics better than Gregg, the former governor. His family has been prominent in state politics for generations. Yet Gregg revealed that Romney paid little attention to his advice there.

They "didn't want me or my organization to do anything," he later said. He actually walked out of the Romney campaign headquarters in Boston in disgust. "My decision was not to get involved in how to run their campaign because they didn't appear to want to know."

It was even worse down in South Carolina. Romney's decision to try to run on the right wing of the party, and to woo social conservatives, always looked desperate. Kranish and Helman reveal, however, that it was taken against the advice of his campaign down there. And they were tearing their hair out.

They knew that South Carolina Republicans would never buy a Massachusetts governor – or a Mormon – as the next Jerry Falwell. All Romney was doing, they argued, was playing to his weakness. Talking so much about abortion, gays, and other social issues mainly just reminded voters of their differences with the governor – and earned him a reputation for weasel words he has never lost.

In early 2007, the South Carolina campaign team wrote a four-page memo to Myers, the national campaign manager, telling them to change course and talk about the economy – the candidate's supposed strength.

"Every time Governor Romney talks about social issues, the flip-flopper accusations have been and will continue to be mentioned," they said. Romney didn't need to be "Mr. Cultural Conservative," they said. He just needed to be "acceptable" to this group. Myers and Romney dismissed their warnings.

This is business strategy 101. If the CEO of a major company ran it like this, he'd be out of a job.

The South Carolina leadership was so unhappy that two members demanded a showdown with the candidate in Columbia, where they told him bluntly that his strategy was backfiring. Romney, reported Kranish and Helman, "thanked them politely and ignored the advice."

No wonder Romney failed in 2008. His social crusade campaign successfully alienated his natural supporters, damaged his brand, and failed to win the voters he was wooing. As a marketing campaign, it was a monumental disaster. Christian conservatives flocked to Mike Huckabee. The former minister (and non-Mormon) took Iowa. Romney's gamble there had failed. Meanwhile it left him vulnerable in New Hampshire. He was hoping that Giuliani would split the moderate vote there with McCain. When Giuliani's campaign ran out of cash, McCain surged ahead and took the Granite State. Romney's campaign in Florida dissolved in confusion. It had spent a small fortune preparing individual mailings for potential voters. They were never sent.

On the night of the New Hampshire loss, Bruce Keough recalls hearing Romney's top campaign staff still discussing what the candidate's "brand" should be.

In the aftermath, commentators sought to blame Romney's failure on the Mormon issue, and in particular on his "failure" to deliver a "big speech" about his religion early on in the campaign. They are probably overstating the issue. However, it was also Romney's decision not to make a speech until it was too late, and then to deliver one that said nothing.

It's too easy to say that his success in 2012 demonstrates his competence. If Mitt Romney had really run his campaign as a top-quality, hands-on CEO, he wouldn't be the Republican nominee today. He might be in the fourth year of his first term as president.

Instead in 2008, at a time of national economic crisis, the two political parties nominated men with absolutely no background in economics. Mitt Romney watched the race on TV at home.

Many people have blamed Romney's problems in two Republican races on his past record on abortion. The media claim his previous "moderate" views supposedly alienated pro-life conservatives. Romney's troubles on the issue, however, have mostly been due to poor strategy and communication. It was his insistence that he had miraculously become "pro-life" at the tender age of 57 – just in time for the Republican presidential race – that left him looking so vulnerable. Instead, all he ever needed to say on the subject was that he opposed Roe v. Wade, and that if elected president, he planned to appoint judges who would overturn it. That's it. Simple.

Such a policy was entirely consistent with his earlier comments on the issue, and left little to attack. As the members of his South Carolina team had said in their memo in 2007, Romney only need to "be acceptable to the pro-life crowd," not its "champion."

Romney actually had a pretty conservative personal story on abortion. According to newspaper reports from 1994, as a leading member of his local Mormon church Romney had intervened to try to dissuade fellow Mormons from having the procedure. How he didn't establish that as his narrative during the Republican primaries is a mystery. Instead he chose to fight his battle by claiming a "miraculous" conversion in the governor's office on Beacon Hill.

Then there was the matter of illegal immigration. In 2007, when Romney was already well into his campaign for the White House, the Boston Globe found that the gardening company that he employed to mow the lawn and trim the hedges at his Belmont estate employed several illegal immigrants. When the paper looked again, almost a year later, they were still there.

"Two hundred fifty million and Mitt still couldn't find an American lawn crew to cut his grass in Belmont?" joked Howie Carr, the conservative Boston radio talk show host. Carr is a Romney supporter, and even he couldn't believe it. Romney first tried blaming it on his sons.

Then he compounded his error by trying to throw haymakers at both Rudy Giuliani and John McCain over the issue of illegal immigration, accusing both of them of supporting "amnesty." It was a foolish gambit, known in boxing as leading with your chin. He was asking for trouble, and he got it.

When Romney accused Giuliani during a debate of running a "sanctuary city," Giuliani shot back with the best line of the race. Romney, he said, had run "a sanctuary mansion at his own home." The laughter turned to applause when the former mayor added that when Romney was governor of Massachusetts, his state troopers couldn't even "catch the illegal immigrants that were working at his mansion." McCain, meanwhile, scornfully suggested Romney "get out that varmint gun of his and chase those Guatemalans off his lawn."

Sometimes Romney's errors were so unforced you wondered if he had prepared for the race at all. During a debate in 2007, when he was asked if he would be willing to go to war with Iran, he replied that first he'd have to consult his lawyers. Even Chris Matthews, host on the liberal MSNBC, asked: "What are these, the Miranda rights for Iran?"

In the summer of 2012 he was kept on the ropes by the

Democrats over his taxes. He could have avoided the problems completely with some basic advanced planning.

Beltway pundits insist that Mitt Romney has "grown" as a candidate, and is so much better in 2012 than he was in 2008. Never mind the question of whether he should still have a lot of growing to do in his chosen profession at the age of 65. The more immediate question is whether it is really true.

Yes, Mitt Romney secured the Republican nomination in 2012. Yes, he has got what he wanted. But look at how.

In January, ABC News political reporter David Muir reported sitting in his hotel room in Jacksonville, Florida, covering the Florida primary and seeing five commercials by Mitt Romney supporters air inside half an hour. All of them were attack ads against his chief rival there, former House Speaker Newt Gingrich. (Three of the five were factually misleading, too.)

During the same period, Muir didn't see a single commercial from the Gingrich side. Not one.

According to the Campaign Media Analysis Group, Romney and his allies aired 8,250 ads in Florida, and all but 200 of those were negative. Newt Gingrich and his supporters were able to put on the air barely a third as many ads.

By the time he had secured the nomination, Romney had already spent about $21 million on media – more than all the other candidates put together, and more than twice as much as his two main rivals put together. And that wasn't the half of it. Romney was ably assisted throughout by his very own hit squad. The "independent" Super PAC Restore Our Future, largely financed by his fellow Wall Streeters and a few wealthy Mormons, spent another $45 million on his behalf. According to the Center for Responsive Politics, that was more than all outside groups had spent by May, 2008.

Restore Our Future didn't spend that money telling

voters why they should support Mitt Romney. They didn't spend it explaining his vision for the future, or what a great guy he was. They spent it destroying his opponents.

Restore Our Future spent just $4.8 million during the primaries on positive commercials for Romney, and $40 million advertising against the others. That included $21 million on attack ads against Rick Santorum and $18 million against Newt Gingrich.

This "independent" body spent more money attacking Gingrich and Santorum than those two candidates spent on their own campaigns. At one point Santorum aired a commercial in response that featured Romney as a 1920s gangster with a "tommy gun", spraying his opponents with mud. It was an appropriate image.

The result was hardly in doubt. Both Santorum and Gingrich went down under a hail of negative commercials.

In the spring of 2008 I met one of Romney's defeated rivals. He argued that Romney's one really smart move in the campaign was to understand early, before anyone else, what the Supreme Court's Citizens United ruling on campaign finance really meant. As a result, Romney was ahead of everyone in making sure that a rich Super PAC was set up to campaign on his behalf. Its attack ads were the decisive factor in his primary victory. "It was like Whack-A-Mole," said the politician. "Any time one of us started doing well in the polls, the Super PAC along and whacked us."

Yet Romney's bruising primary battles with Rick Santorum and Newt Gingrich, and his eventual "triumph," masked what should have been the obvious point: He shouldn't have been in a battle with them at all.

The Republican field in 2012 was among the weakest ever assembled by a major political party. Newt Gingrich and Rick Santorum were unviable in a general election – Gingrich mainly for personal reasons, Santorum for his extreme views on social issues. The other candidates were barely worth mentioning. Herman Cain? Michele Bachmann? Rick Perry?

Yet Mitt Romney struggled to secure the nomination against this field, even after outspending them all by a huge multiple.

He came into this race holding all the cards, too.

Not only did he have a big financial advantage over his competitors, he had a national organization all set up and ready to go. Once again he was so rich he didn't have to hold down a day job, so he was free to spend his entire time, from the day after Barack Obama's election victory in 2008, building his campaign. He had the Republican establishment in the tank. Even Matt Drudge's website The Drudge Report, home base for many conservatives, became a quasi-arm of his campaign. It conveniently unloaded on his rivals, such as Newt Gingrich, at critical moments, splashing negative adverts on behalf of the Romney campaign at the top whenever needed. (As Romney and Gingrich faced off in Florida, wrote the New York Times' Michael Shear, "the conservative Web site led by Matt Drudge has become a virtual campaign arm for Mitt Romney." The result, Shear added, was that many anti-Romney conservatives were up in arms, accusing Drudge of "selling out.") And he had a race where the economy was topic number one. It was tailor made for a candidate with a business background.

In total, from 2006 to the spring of 2012, Federal Election Commission filings show Romney spent $180 million in two election cycles. That money has been spent building campaign organizations, working the grassroots, and marketing his name and his record to Republican primary voters around the country. In the end he barely won the nomination on points. He was on the ropes time and again. In New Hampshire. In Florida. In Michigan.

Sometimes it has seemed that Romney can't even master the basics. Consider, for example, the ongoing trouble he is getting over his tax returns. At the time of writing he has released two years' returns, and is refusing to release any more. The Obama campaign is pounding him mercilessly on this. Romney's father, when he ran for president in 1968, released twelve years'.

But the real issue is not about taxes. It's about competence. Romney has been running for president for at least six years. Yet his tax returns showed almost no planning or preparation for this moment at all.

The candidate and his wife hold millions in an offshore trust in the Cayman Islands, a Caribbean island named by the General Accounting Office as recently as 2008 as a haven of "tax evasion…securities fraud, money laundering, and various other types of fraud." The Romneys have also revealed that they had held money in a Swiss bank account, only closing it down a year earlier because they realized, belatedly, that it might look bad in an election.

It goes further. The Romneys also hold money in obscure hedge funds. These are especially dangerous for a presidential candidate. Hedge funds operate by betting on stocks that they think will do well, and simultaneously betting against the stocks of companies they think are weak and vulnerable. They profit when those companies get into trouble, lay people off, and go out of business. That's the whole point of a "hedge" strategy. Did Romney's funds bet against U.S. stocks during the financial crash? I would be surprised if none of them did. That's what they are supposed to do. That's how they try to protect their investors' wealth in down markets. There is nothing wrong with that. But it's hardly what you want if you are running for president. It won't play in Poughkeepsie.

In November, 2008 Mitt Romney wrote an Op-Ed in the New York Times urging the government not to rescue the collapsing automakers. The headline was blunt: "Let Detroit Go Bankrupt."

Maybe that was the right policy to recommend. And let's

assume Romney did so for entirely honest reasons. But the danger for him is that many hedge funds were betting against GM securities – stocks, bonds and preferreds – at the time. Their investors stood to make money if these securities were wiped out, as they eventually were. Did this include any hedge funds in which Romney was an investor? Would he have known? Even if we assume he did nothing wrong, such funds are an accident waiting to happen for a politician. A smart executive would steer clear.

Meanwhile, the Romneys revealed that although they had earned $42.5 million over the previous two years, they had paid a tax rate of just 14.6%. In 2010, they paid $3 million in taxes on $21.7 million in income, a rate of just 13.9%. A student bussing tables pays more than that, just in FICA taxes.

Romney dumped this amazing political gift into the lap of his opponents in January, 2012, on the night that President Obama had chosen to make "fair" taxes for the rich a major part of his State of the Union Address.

"Right now," the president said that night from the podium, "we're poised to spend nearly $1 trillion more on what was supposed to be a temporary tax break for the wealthiest two percent of Americans. Right now, because of loopholes and shelters in the tax code, a quarter of all millionaires pay lower tax rates than millions of middle-class households."

He added: "Right now, Warren Buffett pays a lower tax rate than his secretary."

The president had even invited Buffett's secretary, Debbie Bosanek, to the speech as his guest. He gestured to her as he made his point.

It was a good piece of theater. The President and the Democrats had been struggling for some time to put a face to the issue that the very wealthy often pay lower tax rates than everyone else.

Ms. Bosanek could have stayed home in Omaha. Mitt

Romney's tax news was ten times better. Over the next week you realized absolutely everybody knew Mitt and Ann had only paid 13.9% tax in 2010. Bartenders. Taxi drivers. Receptionists. Everyone knew about it.

Creating that kind of public awareness through advertising surely would have cost the Democrats tens of millions of dollars. Romney gave it to them for free.

Even Rupert Murdoch, the conservative owner of Fox News (and the Journal), was stunned. "Romney's tax returns might kill his chances," he tweeted. "See the Republican establishment panic now!"

The real lesson of this, however, has largely been overlooked. Romney's financial fancy-dealing probably didn't even save him any money. Why not? Because most of these elaborate financial vehicles just aren't worth it. They cost too much in fees.

Let's do the math. Romney's portfolio is valued at about $250 million. His money is held in a "blind trust" overseen by a partner at Ropes & Gray, one of the top law firms in Boston. These people do not come cheap. A friend who works in Boston's white-shoe legal industry tells me that the fees for managing a portfolio through a blind trust typically start at around 1% of the assets a year, although a portfolio as big as Romney's would get a discount. Even if Romney were only paying half a percent a year, that would come to about $1.3 million.

And this is only the beginning. A look through Romney's statement of personal financial disclosure shows that his portfolio includes dozens of specialized hedge funds and private equity partnerships, including some at Goldman Sachs and Bain Capital.

The fees on these are, quite simply, astronomical. Romney knows that, because he used to be in the business.

I once calculated for MarketWatch that the typical hedge fund charges more than 3% of the assets per year. In the case of private equity, says Oxford's Ludovic Phalippou, the cost is even higher: Closer to 7%, he says.

Romney's personal financial disclosures show that he has somewhere between $30 million and $100 million in these types of high-fee funds. The midpoint is about $65 million. If he's paying just 3% on that money, that's another $2 million in fees. Combined with the 0.5% overall portfolio management fee, that would take him well over $3 million. And these estimates are conservative.

In other words, for all his financial maneuvers, Mitt Romney is almost certainly paying more to his friends at Goldman Sachs, Bain Capital and Ropes & Gray than he is paying to Uncle Sam. "His fees...probably will exceed the taxes that he paid," Don Williamson, executive director of the American University's Kogod Tax Center, and a CPA with thirty years' experience, told me. "The fees for running the blind trust, for managing the portfolio, for the hedge funds and private equity, and for the accountants and the tax preparers...all of those could easily exceed the $3 million [Romney] paid in taxes."

For this Romney gets nothing but headaches. A fool and his money, as they say. He could have saved himself a great deal of trouble, and money, by putting his money in a handful of low-cost funds. It would have made him look very smart, too.

Where is Romney, the supposedly no-nonsense, safe-hands executive, in any of these campaigns?

When Romney ran against Kennedy in 1994, he tried to make an issue out of the senator's tax returns. He demanded that Kennedy release three years of tax returns to prove he had "nothing to hide." Yet eighteen years later, Romney would prove unable to handle the release of his own tax returns without political embarrassment.

When Kennedy pleaded that investments were in a blind trust back then, Romney scornfully shot the defense down. "The blind trust is an age-old ruse," Romney said at the time, according to a 2002 report in the Globe. "You can say to a blind trust, don't invest in properties which would be in conflict of interest, or where the seller might think they're going to get an advantage from me." Yet in 2012 Romney would try to cover for his own embarrassing investments by saying they were in a blind trust.

How do you get surprised by attacks when you've had eighteen years to prepare?

So far in his career, Mitt Romney has run four political campaigns. None has been impressive. Three have been astonishingly inept. It is hardly what we would expect from a high-quality, hands-on executive.

It may be unfair to dwell for too long on his first losing campaign, the 1994 U.S. Senate against Ted Kennedy. Romney was a political novice. Kennedy, of course, was an old pro, and was fighting on his home turf. And it was a long time ago. Yet even then the history is different from what we have been told.

Romney has since claimed that he faced an impossible task, that he was a valiant David taking on an unbeatable Goliath. Yet Kennedy was vulnerable. Six weeks before the election, polls showed Romney was either tied with Kennedy, or even ahead. And it was a good year for Republicans across the country.

As we've seen, Romney helped blow his advantages. He wasn't prepared for Kennedy's attacks on his business record. He went into the critical debate with a fatally casual attitude.

Eight years later, he entered a much easier race with much greater advantages – and nearly blew that too. In 2002, when Romney ran for governor of Massachusetts, he was in a strong position. He faced a weak opponent. The state's economy was struggling. Romney had emerged in triumph from the successful Salt Lake City Olympics. This was when many prominent voices in Boston, across the spectrum, were urging him to come back and run for governor. Rudy Giuliani, then at the peak of his post-9/11 prestige, even campaigned for him. The lights were all green.

He nearly blew the election before it started. While in Salt Lake City he had claimed his home there as his primary residence, in order to save on property taxes. But it threw his eligibility into question for the governor's race in Massachusetts. You have to be resident for seven years before you can run.

When the question broke, it quickly emerged that neither Romney, nor any of his advisers, had thought about the issue for a moment. They initially issued conflicting, and, um, inaccurate, statements. In the end the candidate was only rescued by the State Ballot Commission, which decided – in an example of the kind of judicial activism that Romney usually deplores – that the letter of the Massachusetts constitution was a technicality which could be ignored.

Even after that, and with all his advantages in the race, he made heavy going of it. In the end, after a mediocre campaign, he only scraped out a win by five points. He had to buy the victory. He outspent opponents by a factor of nearly two to one. Millions of that went on negative ads, including a deluge in the final weeks. They would become his signature.

7

A BEGINNER'S GUIDE TO
ROMNEYSPEAK

In June, 2011 the world was introduced to a new economic indicator. Writing in my old paper, the Boston Herald, Mitt Romney announced that the "Obama Misery Index" had just hit a "record high; indeed, it makes even the malaise of the Carter years look like a boom."

What was the Obama Misery Index? No one had ever heard of it before. Romney's campaign headquarters in Boston is a short walk across the Charles River from Harvard, the Massachusetts Institute of Technology, and the National Bureau of Economic Research. But no one at any of those august institutions had ever heard of the OMI.

The phrase recalled Ronald Reagan's famous "Misery Index" charge against Jimmy Carter back in 1980. But Reagan had offered a hard, measurable number: The "Misery Index" was the official unemployment rate added to the official inflation rate. Romney said the Obama Misery Index included a much wider array of inputs:

"unemployment, debt, home foreclosures, and bankruptcies."

Alarmingly, a few months later Romney said the Obama Misery Index "had never been higher," which means it had either plateaued, or gotten even worse, since March.

Factcheck.org was curious about the OMI. So it contacted the Romney campaign to find out how the former Bain consultant was calculating these numbers. Eric Fehrnstrom gave a candid reply. The OMI, he said, had no actual number. "It is a rhetorical reference that encompasses real unemployment, foreclosures, bankruptcies, national debt and *whatever other indicator that Governor Romney wants to use* to illustrate the mess the country finds itself in." (Italics added.) The index, in other words, is whatever Governor Romney says it is. But if that is the case, isn't it always at a record if the governor says so? Does this mean Romney will be able to announce that the OMI has started falling the day after his election?

It is all too easy to laugh at Mitt Romney's peculiar form of political rhetoric. All politicians pander, flip-flop, and talk nonsense. Romney, nonetheless, has taken it to a new level.

He has accused Barack Obama of spending too long at Harvard, even though he actually spent longer there than the president did, and sent several sons there as well. Romney's snarky remark came less than a year after he had hosted a $25,000-a-plate fundraiser at the Harvard club in New York.

He has attacked the influence of Super PACs and negative attack ads in politics while benefiting from them more than anyone. He has attacked the greed of excessive CEO pay, and the Democrats for complaining about it. In 2007, as Democrats criticized President Bush's foreign policy, Romney told Fox's Sean Hannity that "politics ends at the water's edge." Since then he has accused President Obama of pandering to America's enemies and undermining our allies. In May, 2011, he accused the president of "throwing Israel under the bus."

In a debate in Florida in January, 2012 he accused Newt Gingrich of making "repulsive" comments and "the kind of over-the-top rhetoric that has characterized American politics for too long." When he bowed out of the 2008 race he warned that if Barack Obama or Hillary Clinton were elected president, America would "surrender to terror."

Romney has made speeches denouncing "East Coast elites," then boarded a jet back to Boston. He bragged during the 2008 race that he had "no lobbyists running my campaign," only to admit, after he was challenged by Glen Johnson of the Associated Press, that it only meant his actual campaign manager – at the time, Beth Myers – wasn't a lobbyist.

Questioned about guns by a voter in New Hampshire, Romney absurdly claimed that he had been hunting "little varmints" all his life. (Joan Venocchi, the columnist at the Boston Globe, expressed the general skepticism best: "Trust Mitt Romney to shoot himself in the foot with a gun he doesn't own.")

In a televised interview with CNN's Wolf Blitzer on January 13, 2008, Romney said as president he would intervene "aggressively" in the housing crisis to prevent unnecessary foreclosures, "so that we don't dump housing product in the housing market and cause a further reduction in housing prices."

In October, 2011, he told the Las Vegas Review-Journal that the reason the housing crisis was dragging on was because the Obama administration had foolishly intervened in foreclosures. They have "slow-walked the foreclosure process," he said, "and as a result we still have a foreclosure overhang." His solution: "Don't try and stop the foreclosure process. Let it run its course and hit the bottom."

Some of this is harmless, or even funny. Who cares if

Mitt Romney, like Elmer Fudd, wants to pretend he hunts "little varmints" (and wabbits)? Who cares if he wants to make himself look ridiculous by attacking Obama for going to Harvard?

Yet Romney's rhetoric is also a serious matter, because it goes way beyond accusations of "flip-flopping," or questions about whether he is "really" pro-choice or pro-life. Mitt Romney's use and abuse of political rhetoric raises deeper questions.

In 2007, as he left the governor's office in Massachusetts and prepared his first run for the White House, a document leaked to the Boston Globe showed how Mitt Romney's campaign was approaching the presidential race: Like it was marketing a product. The PowerPoint presentation looked at the competing "brands" of the rivals, and sketched out ideas to create "Brand Romney." Among the suggestions: Romney should differentiate himself by attacking high-profile bogeymen that were hated within the Republican party. These included "jihadism," such as the terrorists who attacked America on 9/11. Others on the list included "Hillary Clinton," "Hollywood liberals," and "France." Oh, and "Massachusetts."

Mitt Romney's background is not in politics. It is in business. He spent his early adult life studying business administration at Harvard, and then applying the theories and techniques he had learned as a consultant, first at the Boston Consulting Group, then at Bain & Co. In the world of business, and product marketing, Romney's approach to communication is perfectly normal.

Product marketing is a far bigger, far more sophisticated business than political marketing. This year U.S. companies are forecast to spend about $200 billion marketing their products. The presidential elections are unlikely to cost 1% of that. How do companies sell detergent, or beer, or sports cars? Try three things, wrote marketing gurus Al Reis and Jack Trout thirty years ago in their classic on the subject,

Positioning. First, don't try to sell a product, just sell the customer. "Concentrate on the perceptions of the prospect...not the reality of the product," they wrote. Reality is meaningless: It's all a battle for the mind. Make whatever "purely cosmetic changes" you need to help those perceptions.

Second, they said, don't compete, differentiate. The market is crowded. Consumers are swamped with advertising. Look for the "hole" or gap in the market and fill it.

Third, they said: Simplify. Strip your message down to the barest essentials and hammer it home, over and over again. "You have to sharpen your message to cut into the mind," they wrote.

It's fine advice, if you're selling soap.

Now look at the political landscape that Mitt Romney faced in the run-up to the 2008 presidential elections. The front-runner was Rudy Giuliani. The second strongest candidate was John McCain. Both were popular with moderate and liberal Republicans. Both were mistrusted on the right of the party.

Never mind that Romney at that time had a reasonable track record as a moderate Republican. Never mind his father's own moderate record. The "gap in the market" was on the extreme right. And that is where he tried to "position" himself.

Mitt Romney devoted enormous energy to presenting himself as an ultra-conservative, a "Reagan conservative," a "values conservative," a pro-life, pro-family values social conservative.

He hammered away at immigration, abortion, and other issues popular with the ultra-conservative wing of the party. Hence his otherwise inexplicable remark, during a debate in South Carolina in May, 2007, "My view is, we ought to double Guantanamo." What does that mean? Nothing. It's just branding.

"Words have no meaning," wrote Ries and Trout: "Truth is irrelevant." Or, as a former Romney aide told Kranish and Helman after the 2008 election, as far as Mitt Romney was concerned, "Everything could always be tweaked, reshaped, fixed, addressed. It was foreign to him on policy issues that core principles mattered – that somebody would go back and say, 'Well, three years ago you said this.' "

During Republican debates you could sometimes catch him trying to cram as many conservative buzzwords into a single answer as he could. During a CNN debate in New Hampshire in June, 2007, Wolf Blitzer, the moderator, asked Romney how he planned to bring more people into the Republican party. Romney, in a reply that only lasted a few seconds, managed to get in, "Ronald Reagan…a strong military…troops…veterans…strong military, strong economy, keeping our taxes down, and strong families and strong family values."

Blitzer thanked him twice and turned to Rudy Giuliani, but before the former mayor could get a word out Romney had remembered two more: "And one more thing: optimism and a vision for the future." It was like a conservatives' version of "buzzword bingo," the game Romney surely played at Harvard Business School.

There is a comic air to this, because Romney is so inept at communication. But it's no joke.

In June, 2006, when the Supreme Court ruled that Guantanamo Bay detainees had rights under U.S. law and the Geneva conventions, Romney was at a small conservative meeting in Atlanta, Georgia. The Associated Press happened to be there. A member of the audience asked Romney, who also has a Harvard law degree, what he thought of the ruling. He replied that he disagreed with it. "To apply the Geneva accords is very strange in my view," he said. "It's hard to understand how a party who's not a nation comes under the Geneva Convention."

If this means anything, it's that a detainee ('party') might not have "rights" because he or she has no nation or state (the language is garbled, but in the context no other explanation seems to fit). This is remarkable. It was especially astonishing from Mitt Romney. Like many in politics, he is fond of reminding voters that "our Creator" gets a special mention in the Declaration of Independence, and is therefore the source of our political rights. "We were endowed by our Creator with our rights," he told a Faith and Freedom Coalition in Fitchburg, Wisconsin in March, 2011. "Not the king, not the state, but our Creator."

If our rights come from our "Creator," and not the "state," then how can detainees at Guantanamo Bay lack rights simply because they are not citizens of a recognized state?

A year later there was a memorable smack-down between Romney and John McCain during a televised debate. Romney, in his repeated attempts to position himself on the right wing of the party, refused to rule out "waterboarding" of terrorism suspects. McCain, a victim of torture himself, came back hard. He said if Romney became president, America would have to withdraw from the Geneva conventions altogether. "My friends, this is what America is all about," McCain said. "This is a defining issue."

In November, 2011, during a debate on CNBC, Romney blamed the housing crisis on the federal government, Fannie Mae and Freddie Mac, and on federal programs for the poor. "Barney Frank and Chris Dodd told banks that they had to give loans to people who couldn't afford to pay them back," he thundered. The audience cheered.

This is patent nonsense, and Mitt Romney knows it. He was playing to the basest elements of the party.

Blaming the federal government, Fannie Mae and Barney Frank for the financial crisis is popular with some on the far right. Money manager Barry Ritholtz, author of the top financial blog The Big Picture, calls it "The Big Lie."

Ritholtz points out that all the serious economic studies of the crisis have debunked it. The explanation, however, creates an easy scapegoat for people on the far right. It lets "deregulation" and "free markets" off the hook. Importantly, it is also racial code: The federal programs being blamed are those that sought to encourage homeownership among the poor, such as the Community Reinvestment Act. The CRA was passed decades ago to stop the "redlining" of ethnic minority neighborhoods. So those feckless "people" that got the soft loans, thanks to Barney Frank – well, we know who they are, right?

In March, 2006, Romney told Bloomberg News then that the country's eleven million illegal immigrants "are not going to be rounded up and box-carred out...We need to begin a process of registering those people, some being returned, and some beginning the process of applying for citizenship and establishing legal status," he said. It was a line he repeated elsewhere, for instance in an interview in the Lowell Sun in Massachusetts.

Yet when John McCain, Rudy Giuliani and Newt Gingrich took similar lines years later, he would merrily tar them with the "amnesty" brush. In December, 2007, reports Factcheck.org, a Romney commercial in New Hampshire accused McCain of supporting "amnesty" and added that McCain had "voted to allow illegals to collect Social Security," a total absurdity. Romney, when pressed, said he didn't know about the commercial.

At a CNN debate in November, 2011, Newt Gingrich urged Republicans to take a humane approach to dealing with illegal immigration. Mitt Romney pounced, calling Gingrich's proposals equal to amnesty. After the debate Fehrnstrom took the line further: "Mitt Romney is against amnesty, and Newt Gingrich made it very clear he was for amnesty," he said.

George Romney had, famously, walked out of the 1964 Republican convention in San Francisco because he felt Barry Goldwater was pandering to the worst elements of the party. The former Michigan governor never lived long enough to see his son outflank Newt Gingrich on the right.

Now consider Romney's changing stance on the issue that made him popular with social conservatives: Gay marriage.

Early in his career, when running for office in Massachusetts, Romney had been very happy to court the state's gay vote. In 1994 he had told the Log Cabin Republicans, the gay Republican organization, that he would prove a better champion for equality than Ted Kennedy. In 2002, Romney's campaign printed pink leaflets for Boston's Gay Pride weekend saying "Mitt and Kerry" wished them a "Great Pride Weekend!"

When the Massachusetts Supreme Judicial Court ruled in favor of gay marriage in November, 2003, Romney's initial reaction was to oppose the move, but to support civil unions as an alternative. "I believe," he wrote in a statement, that offering "the benefits, obligations, rights and responsibilities" of marriage, but "perhaps under a different name, would be in conformity with their decision…Under that opinion, I believe a civil union type provision would be sufficient."

It was what you would have expected from someone who ran as a moderate conservative, and whose inaugural address had promised to defend people's rights, "regardless of gender, sexual orientation, or race."

Over the next nineteen months, as his national ambitions beckoned and his marketing plan developed, he would back away from that. By June, 2005, Romney would abandon his support for a constitutional amendment which instituted civil unions instead of gay marriage, and would instead throw his weight behind another amendment that would forbid both. Over the next year he would join extreme social conservatives, such as Tony Perkins of the Family Research Council, in an increasingly strident campaign.

Romney's only concession on the issue has been to say that the campaign against gay marriage should not be taken as the starting gun for a wider campaign of intolerance or hatred. He told the National Review in December, 2006, "I've opposed same-sex marriage, but I've opposed unjust discrimination against anyone, for racial or religious reasons, or for sexual preference." It's a statement which is self-serving and largely meaningless. Imagine a politician saying otherwise. (And why the distinction about "unjust" discrimination?)

He's been willing to skirt the line, too. In November, 2005, speaking at a convention of the ultra-conservative Federalist Society in Washington, D.C., the governor launched an extraordinary personal attack on chief justice Margaret Marshall and the others on the Massachusetts Supreme Judicial Court. They had, Romney said, put "the social proclivities" of their friends and the "communities they socialize in" above "the law [and] the values that were placed in the constitution."

"Social" proclivities? This is code. Romney came close to accusing Marshall of hanging around with too many homos. It was a disgraceful remark from a sitting governor. The irony was that Marshall had even been appointed by Governor Weld, a Republican.

What was Romney's game? Joe Cannon, an old friend of Romney's and the chairman of the Utah Republican Party, revealed it in February, 2005.

Cannon told the Boston Globe that he had advised Romney that a public fight with gays would be good for him politically. It would help him curry favor with the most right-wing primary voters in the red states. "The more he gets bashed by gay advocates, the better that is for him in terms of electoral politics," Cannon said. The delegates from red states, he added, were 90-10 on the issue.

Romney's ideological figleaf for his campaign against gays getting married was the issue of "the children." To a conservative Republican group in Spartanburg, South Carolina in early 2005 he said the court ruling had "struck a blow against the family…The court forgot that marriage is first and foremost about nurturing and developing children." At a church-based rally against gay marriage in October, 2006, reported the Associated Press, he thundered that "The price of same-sex marriage is paid by the children." What the judges ignored, he said, "is that marriage is not primarily about adults; marriage is about the nurturing and development of children."

No explanation has ever been forthcoming about how the marriage of two homosexuals endangers other marriages, or the children of them. If marriage is only about children, should sterile couples, or those past child-bearing age, be forbidden to marry? Should couples who do not have children be forcibly divorced? And why should gay marriage threaten the stability of other marriages anyway?

Romney is a former strategy consultant. He's a numbers guy. Has he crunched them on this issue? According to the latest reading by the U.S. Census, the divorce rate in Massachusetts in 2000, before the Attack of the Marrying Gays, was 2.5 a year per 1,000 people. In 2009 it was…2.2 per 1,000. In the wake of the Supreme Judicial Court's ruling, the number of marriages breaking up has actually fallen sharply. So much for Gaymaggedon.

Massachusetts continues to have the lowest divorce rate in the country. In conservative South Carolina the divorce rate is 3 per 1,000, and in Joe Cannon's Utah, 3.6. A couple in Utah is far more likely to divorce than a couple in Massachusetts.

Romney was being even more cynical than national voters may have realized. Boston politics insiders laugh knowingly whenever they hear some of his more pious and sanctimonious rhetoric. Not everyone that Mitt Romney has hired for positions of importance, in his administration or his campaign, meets this standard of "traditional morality" or "the sanctity of marriage." Romney knows all about it. He doesn't seem to care.

What Romney has never seemed to grasp is that in selling his soul to gain the world he risks ending up with neither. That's what happened in 2008, when he lost a dishonest race against McCain where an honest one probably would have succeeded. And in 2012 his brand is badly tarnished.

On no other issue has Mitt Romney's "positioning" been more apparent than that of abortion.

Many call it flip-flopping. However, from one point of view, Mitt Romney's position on abortion has been consistent: Throughout his political career, from 1994 through the 2012 primaries, he has always offered the position on abortion that matched his target voters. He hasn't been "pro-choice" or "pro-life." He's been "pro-winning the election." The customer, as they say in business, is always right.

In 1994, when he ran against Ted Kennedy for the U.S. Senate, he faced a Massachusetts electorate that was deeply pro-choice. According to Ronald Scott's biography, *Romney*, pollster Richard Wirthlin showed Romney that "no candidate who opposed a woman's right to make her own reproductive choices would ever get elected to a statewide political office in the Commonwealth of Massachusetts."

In this election Romney told the voters he was pro-choice. "I believe that abortion should be safe and legal in this country," he said during a debate with Kennedy. "I believe that since Roe v. Wade has been the law for 20 years we should sustain and support it."

Romney even went further. When Kennedy questioned his sincerity, Romney responded by sharing the deeply personal family tragedy that had, apparently, convinced him that you should not make abortion illegal. Back when he was a teenager, and abortion was still illegal, a "dear, close family relative that was very close to me" had died during an illegal backstreet abortion.

"Since that time," he said, "my mother and my family have been committed to the belief that we can believe as we want but we will not force our belief on others on the matter, and you will not see me wavering on that."

The Romneys were photographed that summer with a former president of Planned Parenthood at a political event in Scituate, a waterfront town just south of Boston. (The photograph later turned up in the Boston Herald.) Ann Romney cut a check to Planned Parenthood.

Fast forward eight years, and once again Romney was facing the Massachusetts electorate. Once again he was pro-choice. He told the Republican convention, reported the Boston Globe at the time, "I respect and will fully protect a woman's right to choose. That choice is a deeply personal one, and the women of our state should make it based on their beliefs, not mine and not the government's."

In a questionnaire distributed by a pro-choice organization, he added that he favored Medicaid funding for women who were too poor to afford abortions on their own. And when Romney's opponents tried to raise doubts in the minds of voters, Fehrnstrom, Romney's spokesman, grew exasperated. He told the Boston Globe in March that Romney's position on abortion, "which he has stated and restated," was "exactly the same position as any other pro-choice politician."

In the fall of 2004, after his successful, high-profile national role attacking John Kerry on behalf of the Bush-Cheney campaign, Romney was being talked about as a potential Republican presidential candidate for 2008. There was a problem. The GOP base was overwhelmingly pro-life. They would be very unlikely to accept a pro-choice candidate for president. "A pro-abortion [sic] candidate would cause civil war within the party," Tom McClusky, a senior figure at the Family Research Council, told the Boston Globe's Frank Phillips in November, 2004. Paul Weyrich, chairman of the Free Congress Foundation, a conservative think-tank in Washington, agreed. "I tell you there would be a civil war," he said. McClusky called Romney "an advocate of abortion." Furthermore, when viewed from a purely marketing perspective, Giuliani was already occupying the pro-choice position in the "marketplace."

Within days, a miracle occurred. Mitt Romney, after a lifetime spent pro-choice, suddenly became pro-life. He himself said the miraculous transformation took place in the governor's office on Beacon Hill, in Boston, on November 9, 2004.

It must have been quite a moment: "And as he journeyed, he came near Damascus: and suddenly there shined round about him a light from heaven," as it says in the Acts of the Apostles. "And he fell to the earth, and heard a voice saying unto him, Saul, Saul, why persecutest thou me? And he said, Who art thou, Lord? And the Lord said, I am Jesus whom thou persecutest." The men who were traveling with Saul, says the Bible, "stood speechless, hearing a voice, but seeing no man."

The Miracle on Beacon Hill, it seems, was more prosaic. Romney's conversion took place quietly, during a conversation about stem-cell research with Harvard professor Douglas A. Melton. (The professor, incidentally, disputes Romney's description of their conversation. He didn't see any lights, or hear any voices, either.)

Since that time, Romney says, he has been pro-life – and not just moderately, either. In March, 2006, his press secretary Julie Teer said he would have even signed an extreme anti-abortion law passed in South Dakota, which (until overturned by voters) banned abortions even in the case of rape or incest, although another spokesman later backpedalled on the more extreme provisions. "I am firmly pro-life," Romney told voters during a debate in New Hampshire in June, 2011. "I believe in the sanctity of life from the very beginning until the very end."

Romney insists his view changed fundamentally as a result of that meeting in November, 2004. Yet three months later, in February, 2005, while he was still considering running for re-election in Massachusetts, he told the Boston Globe that he didn't like to describe himself as pro-life.

"I don't really describe my position in one hyphenated word," he said. "I describe the same thing I have for some time during this last campaign, that is that I personally do not favor abortion. I'm personally pro-life, if you will. But as the governor of the Commonwealth, I will not change the pro-choice laws of the Commonwealth."

He added: "I will support them, sustain them, keep them in place. And we haven't changed the laws, and I will not change the laws as long as I'm governor."

Romney said not merely that he would accept the Massachusetts abortion laws as a matter of fact, but that he would even "support them" and "sustain them." How are such comments compatible with a miraculous conversion the preceding November? They aren't, of course.

No wonder seriously pro-life voters refused to trust him – while pro-choice voters felt so betrayed that the Republican Majority for Choice actually ran commercials against him in Iowa and New Hampshire in 2007, even though most of his opponents were even less pro-choice. "If we weren't so betrayed by the dishonesty of Mitt Romney's actions," co-chair Jennifer Blei Stockman told the Associated Press, "we would not be running ads."

Who is the real Mitt Romney? What does he actually believe? Does such a person even exist? On the issue of abortion, voters got a fascinating glimpse behind the candidate's political veil in a radio studio in Des Moines, Iowa, in December, 2007.

Romney was a guest of Jan Mickelson, the very conservative talk-show host in the state. After the program went off the air, the pair continued their conversation about abortion. In this more private setting, Romney opened up much more on the subject than he had on the campaign trail. The entire conversation was picked up by a studio camera and microphone that had been left on. You can see the whole thing on YouTube.

In the ten-minute conversation, Mickelson took Romney to task for his past pro-choice views (which Mickelson wrongly calls "pro-abortion"). Romney responded with a passionate and convincing explanation of why a Mormon could or would be pro-choice, despite their own religion's strictures against abortion. While the Latter-day Saints were "vehemently" against abortion in most cases, Romney said, "We also vehemently believe that other people should be able to make their own choices…. I accept all my faith but I don't impose all of my faith's beliefs on you!"

When Mickelson pushed back, and insisted that Mormons should all be pro-life, Romney became agitated. "That's not what my church says!" he shouted. "That's not what my church says! That's not what my church says! There are leaders of my church that are pro-choice!"

When Massachusetts senator John Kerry ran for president in 2004, he was widely accused of being a flip-flopper for his changing positions on the war in Iraq. Kerry never successfully rebuffed the charges. It is a great irony that one of those people accusing John Kerry of flip-flopping back then was Mitt Romney, then his state's governor and a point-man for the Bush-Cheney campaign.

"I have some perspective on the man," Romney said to a Republican group in Michigan in April, 2004. "He's a good person. He's a friendly person. Shake his hand and say hello and have a nice conversation. But interestingly enough, if you talk to him about the issues, you have difficulty understanding exactly where he stands."

8

A MATTER OF FAITH

The campaign began with a bang.

It was September, 1994. Mitt Romney had just won the Republican primary for the Senate race. Ted Kennedy, his opponent in the general election, had responded by throwing a political grenade. He had publicly challenged Romney over his Mormon faith, noting that until 1978 the church had been explicitly racist. Kennedy wanted to know where Romney stood on the matter.

Romney responded in kind. He called a snap press conference and fired back. Even his father, George Romney, joined the fight. The younger Romney insisted his religion remain out of bounds. He invoked the memory of Kennedy's late brother, John, who had fought religious prejudice as a Roman Catholic during the 1960 presidential race, and who had made a celebrated speech then defending the separation of church and politics.

"In my view the victory that John Kennedy won was not for just 40 million Americans who were born Catholics,"

Romney declared. "It was for all Americans of all faiths. And I am sad to say that Ted Kennedy is trying to take away his brother's victory."

Romney Senior weighed in. "I think it is absolutely wrong to keep hammering on the religious issues," he said. "And what Ted is trying to do is bring it into the picture." The elder Romney, a governor when JFK ran for office, added: "I think what Jack Kennedy did was absolutely right."

Romney's move to claim Jack Kennedy's mantle was a smart one. He killed the Mormon issue for the election. Both the conservative Boston Herald, and the liberal Boston Globe, rallied to Romney's side. It's a gambit Romney has played over and again in the years since.

Mitt Romney is not merely a Mormon. He is an active and devout member of the Church of Jesus Christ of Latter-day Saints, a self-described "leader" in his church, and he comes from one of its oldest and best-known families. He has served as a lay priest and bishop in Boston. Anyone who has caught him talking about his religion understands how engaged he is. From 1966 to 1968, he spent thirty months as a missionary in France.

As one of his former advisers on Beacon Hill told me, "the thing to remember about Mitt Romney is that he's basically Mormon royalty." One of the major roads into Salt Lake City is named after an ancestor. If you read the famous Mormon proclamation of 1978, where the top church elders announced the end of the race bar, you'll see three signatures at the bottom. The second is that of G. Marion Romney, a distant cousin.

Romney has always insisted that his religion is off limits in elections.

When he first ran for public office, in 1994, he was accused by a Republican primary opponent, John Lakian, of wielding the Jack Kennedy line like a red flag, waving prying eyes away from any issue by saying, in effect, "that's private, that's my religion."

During the race for governor in 2002 it emerged that he had made a $1 million (tax-deductible) donation to Brigham Young University – aka Mormon U – in Salt Lake City a few years earlier, even though the university explicitly discriminated against homosexual students, and had expelled students accused of homosexual conduct. Romney demanded that the issue be ruled out of bounds. "BYU is a religiously oriented university," he told the Globe in October, 2002. "I just don't think religion should be part of a campaign…It's a religious institution. Sorry."

When he ran for the White House five years later, he tried to draw the same line. "I don't like coming on the air and having you come after me and my church," he snapped at Jan Mickelson in their December, 2007 open-mike argument. "I'm not running as a Mormon, and I get a little tired of coming on a show like yours and having it all about Mormon."

Many evangelical Christians consider Mormonism little better than a cult. It has proven a problem for Romney during two Republican campaigns. He tried to ignore the issue for months. However, in the fall of 2007 he began hemorrhaging evangelical Christian votes in Iowa to former minister Mike Huckabee. So he followed in Jack Kennedy's footsteps, almost literally. Kennedy had given his big speech on religion to a group of Protestant ministers in Houston. In December, 2007, just weeks before voting began in Iowa, Romney also went to Houston, to give his speech on religion to a handpicked audience at the George H. W. Bush Presidential Library. As in 1994, he conjured up the former president's ghost.

"Almost 50 years ago another candidate from Massachusetts explained that he was an American running for president, not a Catholic running for president," Romney said. "Like him, I am an American running for president. I do not define my candidacy by my religion. A person should not be elected because of his faith nor should he be rejected because of his faith."

He continued: "Let me assure you that no authorities of my church, or of any other church for that matter, will ever exert influence on presidential decisions. Their authority is theirs, within the province of church affairs, and it ends where the affairs of the nation begin."

He argued that in his past public role he had already shown he would keep his religion out of his public role.

"As governor, I tried to do the right as best I knew it, serving the law and answering to the Constitution," he said. "I did not confuse the particular teachings of my church with the obligations of the office and of the Constitution – and of course, I would not do so as president. I will put no doctrine of any church above the plain duties of the office and the sovereign authority of the law."

Romney's move to invoke Kennedy seemingly left evangelical voters in Iowa unmoved. A few weeks later they turned out for Huckabee.

Romney has continued to struggle to win over some conservative evangelicals. What about the rest of the electorate? Mitt Romney wants to draw a veil over his religion, but that gives rise to two questions. First, does it make sense to ignore a candidate's religion, whether it be Romney's, or Barack Obama's, or someone else's? Second, if Romney wants to insist on a rigid divide between religion and politics, does he actually practice what he preaches?

Let's go back to what Jack Kennedy said. His 1960 speech is a legend in political history. "I am not the Catholic candidate for president," he famously told the Houston ministers, "I am the Democratic Party's candidate for president, who happens also to be a Catholic." Kennedy said he believed in an America "where the separation of church and state is absolute, where no Catholic prelate would tell the president (should he be Catholic) how to act and no Protestant minister would tell his parishioners for whom to vote," and where "no religious body seeks to impose its will directly or indirectly upon the general populace or the public acts of its officials." The president, he added, should be "responsible to all groups and obligated to none." It was, in short, a two way street. Politics had no place in religion – and religion had no place in politics.

Most people would agree that fine matters of theology have no place in a presidential race. We would not expect a presidential debate about the relative merits of transubstantiation or consubstantiation, the existence of Purgatory, or of how many angels can dance on the head of a pin. During their open-mike argument, Romney and Iowa's Mickelson debated whether Jesus' Second Coming would take place in Jerusalem or Missouri. It's hard to see this being a major issue in a presidential election. (How would you vote?)

But someone who is devout will draw their values and their worldview from their faith. What is God's plan for the poor? When is a war justified? What are our obligations to our fellow men and women? If Heaven exists, does it really matter that much what happens on Earth? What should we do about suffering? What should we do about sin? It is hardly possible to govern without dealing with all these issues every day. If someone is guided on these matters by their faith, isn't that something the voters ought to know about? Isn't that a subject for legitimate debate?

How, after all, could anyone understand the Bush administration without understanding President Bush's very conservative branch of Protestantism? After 9/11, the President frequently referred to Al Qaida terrorists as "evildoers." The media, which is mostly secular, never seemed quite interested in why he had chosen this peculiar word, or why he kept repeating it. But anyone who has read the Bible knows it is drawn from the King James version of the Old Testament. Evildoers turn up all the time. The righteous smite them. If you hadn't read the book, you were probably taken by surprise by the administration's foreign policy after 9/11. A lot of people were.

Mitt Romney has said that God is central, not merely to his religious life, but to his political philosophy as well. "We are," he frequently reminds voters, "one nation, under God." As he told the Faith and Freedom Coalition in Fitchburg, Wisconsin in March, 2012, "We were endowed by our Creator with our rights…Not the king, not the state, but our Creator."

Campaigning in Iowa in January, he implied that Barack Obama's social and economic policies were somehow sacrilegious. "I think President Obama wants to make us a European-style welfare state," said Romney, according to ABC News. "They'll substitute envy for ambition. And they'll poison the very spirit of America and keep us from being one nation under God." Challenged by Matt Lauer on NBC the next day, Romney said that "dividing America based on the 99 percent versus 1 percent" was "entirely inconsistent with the concept of one nation under God."

Never mind the Laffer Curve or Keynesian economics. It would be fascinating to know on which passages of scripture Mitt Romney is basing these economic policies, or others he proposes. But even though they are central, apparently we are not allowed to ask.

How can these not be political questions?

In July, 1994, while Romney was running for the Senate, he was credibly accused of describing homosexuality as "perverse" in a meeting at his Mormon Church. The Boston Globe quoted one witness by name, former church official Rick Rawlins. It reported that three others had corroborated the story, though they were not willing to be quoted by name. Romney denied the story only in part. He said he had not used the word "perverse" to describe homosexuality, but agreed that he had called homosexual acts, as well as heterosexual sex outside of marriage, "acts of evil."

"I specifically said they should avoid homosexuality and they should avoid heterosexual relations outside of marriage," he said in an interview with the Globe. He then, as usual, insisted that this was a purely religious matter and he drew a veil over further discussion.

His argument allowed him to claim that he was not really discriminating against any one group. He actively courted the gay vote during his 1994 election campaign, arguing, in a letter to one organization, that he would be a better champion of equality than Kennedy.

Yet ten years later, when Romney was governor, after the Massachusetts Supreme Court ruled that homosexual marriage must be legalized, he chose to lead the fight against it. "I agree with 3,000 years of recorded history. I disagree with the Supreme Judicial Court of Massachusetts," Romney said immediately after the ruling. A year later, reported the Globe, in a speech to Iowa Republicans in October, 2004 he called the ruling "a blow to the entire nation" and urged a constitutional amendment to ban same sex marriages. As governor he even resuscitated an obscure old law, dating back to 1913 and once used to block interracial marriages for out-of-state couples, to prevent gays from coming to Massachusetts to tie the knot.

The two points, a decade apart, add up to much more than the sum of the parts. If all sex outside marriage is "evil," and yet gays, alone, are forbidden to marry, then it must follow that gays are – uniquely and inevitably – condemned to evil.

Why did Romney take such a strong stand against gay marriage? Electoral politics and his own national ambitions played their role, as mentioned earlier. Yet how far was religion also an influence? The Mormon church explicitly condemns homosexuality. "The Church opposes homosexual behavior," it says on the church's official website, although it adds that it offers "understanding and respect" for those who experience "same-gender attraction" so long as they remain celibate. It has even suggested Mormons treat their gay friends warily.

The Mormon church has taken a vehement stand in the nationwide fight against gay marriage. Mormons played a major role in 2008 to support Proposition 8 in California, banning same-sex marriages there. Church "Elder" Lance Wickman, in a statement in 2006, put the official argument succinctly. There cannot be "two marriages, co-existing side by side, one heterosexual and one homosexual," he said. "The hard reality…is that marriage like all other institutions can only have one definition without changing the very character of the institution."

If Mitt Romney or the Mormon church were merely fighting for the right of Mormon temples not to perform same-sex marriages, this might legitimately be a private matter. That, however, was not what they were doing. They were – and are – fighting to deny gays the right to civil marriages. Elder Wickman's explanation, that when a magistrate marries two gays in Provincetown, Massachusetts it undermines the marriage of two straight Mormons in Salt Lake City, wouldn't withstand five seconds' scrutiny. Any candidate for a job at Bain Capital who produced logic like that in an interview would be shown the door. As noted earlier, the divorce rate in Utah is already 64% higher than the one in Massachusetts.

How are these not matters for public debate? How is it that voters are told that they are not to ask these questions, and not to probe the candidate's views?

Mitt Romney's ties to the Mormon church have other public effects. He supports the Mormon church and its affiliates with millions of dollars in tax-deductible contributions every year. During the second primary debate in Florida in January, 2012, he said his tax rate "plus my charitable contributions" would be about 40% of his income for 2011. However, conflating his taxes and his contributions was chicanery. These are different things. Money given to the Mormon church does not pay for roads, air traffic control, defense, police or Medicaid. When someone makes a taxable donation, they are by definition reducing the amount of their contribution to social costs.

If Romney gave millions to secular charities, we would be free to ask about them. Why not religious ones?

There is another hot-button issue about the Mormon church that cannot be avoided.

Until June, 1978, when the Prophet of the Mormon church claimed a new revelation, the Church of Jesus Christ of Latter-day Saints was racist. It was not merely racist in the de facto way that many people were back then (and today, for that matter), but it was explicitly racist as a matter of policy. Black skin, said the Book of Mormon, was the result of God's curse. "And he had caused the cursing to come upon them, yea, even a sore cursing, because of their iniquity," it says in the second Book of Nephi. "For behold…wherefore, as they were white, and exceedingly fair and delightsome, that they might not be enticing unto my people the Lord God did cause a skin of blackness to come upon them." Those with black skin, it continued, were "an idle people, full of mischief and subtlety." They "shall be loathsome unto thy people, save they shall repent of their iniquities," it warned, and "they shall be a scourge unto thy seed."

The church treated black people as second class people. They were forbidden from the priesthood – a much wider group than in most religions – and from many other official functions.

What did Mitt Romney do about that, if anything? He has said that the day the church changed its ruling was one of the happiest of his life. He heard the news on the car radio while driving by a lake west of Boston, and he pulled over he was so happy. That's material. But what about before? Did he reject the church's teachings? Did he consider them merely an obnoxious but irrelevant oddity, the way most Christians view certain parts of Leviticus? Did he speak out against them? If not, why not? And if he didn't reject the church's teachings, when did he change his views, and why?

These are reasonable questions. Apparently, however, we are never to know the answer, even before being asked to vote for Mitt Romney for president in November. And that's because all of this happened behind that magical "veil" which is deemed to shield everything related to religion from the public gaze.

Many will reply that this was all a long time ago. Things were different then. And so they were. Most religions have some peculiar or offensive views buried somewhere. But Mitt Romney was no mere bystander and he was not a neophyte. From 1966 to 1968, while the discrimination against people of color was in place, he had been a missionary for the Mormon church in France. (This earned him a deferment from the Vietnam draft.) He had been working hard to convert people into the faith. By 1978 Romney was already thirty-one years old. He was eagerly rising up through the hierarchy. He was within three years of becoming a lay priest.

No comparable aspect of a candidate's life is treated this way. During the most recent Republican race, Texas governor Rick Perry was even forced to answer questions about a rock on his parents' ranch that had once had a racist inscription on it. Yet Romney's work proselytizing for a racist religion is apparently off limits. In the 1970s, the Mormon church spent a fortune campaigning against the Equal Rights Amendment. In 1979 it even excommunicated the head of Mormons for ERA. We aren't to know what Romney thought of that either. When the Globe asked him in a written questionnaire in 1994, he refused to answer.

Romney's insistence that we draw a veil over his religion

is dubious enough. But does he even practice what he preaches? He is fond of quoting Jack Kennedy, and insisting on a wall of separation between church and state. Does he respect that wall himself?

In September, 2006 Romney was finishing his term as governor of Massachusetts and preparing his first run for the White House. The candidate – or his inner circle – was caught trying to use the Latter-day Saints network to help his presidential campaign. Emails surfaced from one of Romney's operatives, Don Stirling, revealing secret meetings in Salt Lake City between the campaign and top figures in the Mormon establishment. Some of them involved the candidate's son, Josh. The meetings focused on how some aspects of the Mormon network might be worked to help a Romney campaign. The plan was called "MVP," for "Mutual Values and Priorities." MVP usually stands for Most Valuable Player. In this case it really stood for: The Mormon Votes Plan. According to the email, church "Elder" Jeffrey Holland, one of the twelve "Apostles" who help run the church, was deeply involved – indeed he was described as "coordinating these matters," and he even hosted the second meeting. The Boston Globe, which broke the story, sent reporters to Salt Lake City and they observed the meeting attendees entering the building. Perhaps most explosively of all, the emails said that Holland in turn had spoken about the matter to the Prophet himself, church president Gordon Hinckley, "who voiced no objections."

The news caused an outcry. In the days that followed, the Romney campaign offered a comic-opera rerun of the old Richard Nixon playbook.

First they tried to blame it on a single "overenthusiastic" operative, Don Stirling, who had allegedly acted on his own and had "overstepped his bounds." Then Mitt Romney tried to blame it on a vendetta by the liberal media. "There are two factions of reporters where I come from in

Massachusetts," he told a crowd of Republican activists in Florida, where he was busy campaigning for the midterm elections. "We have Hillary-loving, Ted Kennedy apologists – and we have the liberals."

Romney's remarks were as tacky as they were inaccurate. But they played well to the local Republican audience, who hooted and cheered.

Finally, when these two defenses of the MVP program had failed, the Romney campaign resorted to the old failsafe. A loyal friend fell on his sword. Kem Gardner, a friend of Romney's for twenty years and a key figure in the meetings, gave an interview with the soft Salt Lake City Tribune, in which he said the whole thing was his fault, and it was really all just a big misunderstanding anyway.

The confused and contradictory reactions gave the story extra credence. And so did Romney's initial, unguarded responses when he was first asked about it. "Clearly, I'm going to raise money from people I know," he said with some surprise, "and that includes BYU [Brigham Young University] alums, people of my church," as well as people of "other churches," Harvard Business School graduates, and so on. Fair enough, you might argue. But no one, including Mitt Romney, would ever suggest that his connection, say, to Harvard Business School was somehow off limits to voters.

Apparently Romney saw nothing wrong with tapping the vast Mormon network – even while simultaneously demanding that his religion, and his access to the vast Mormon tax-privileged structure, must somehow remain exempt from all political scrutiny. It's as if Kennedy, after giving his speech in Houston in 1960, had then flown to Rome to see how the Roman Catholic Church in America might be mobilized on his behalf.

Political news is like an iceberg. We only get to see about 10% of what's there (if that). Given what leaked out of the tightly knit Mormon club about their ties to the Romney campaign, it is tempting to wonder what else was going on that we couldn't see. As far back as 1994, Paul Rolly, political columnist for the Salt Lake City Tribune, remarked on how much fund-raising Mitt Romney was doing in Utah for his Senate campaign. In his 2002 campaign for governor of Massachusetts, Romney received checks from 5,300 donors from outside the state, reports the Massachusetts Office of Campaign and Political Finance. They raised $1.3 million. Much of this came from out west, including more than $100,000 from Utah. That may not sound like much by the standards of modern federal elections, but it was a great deal for a mere statewide race ten years ago, especially as Massachusetts limited each donor to $500. Why were so many people in Utah so engaged in a governor's race across the country? Romney got funds from 1,165 people in the state. Shannon O'Brien, the Massachusetts state treasurer and his chief opponent in the race, got funds from two. The total raised: $110.

These donations gave Romney an advantage. He was losing the 2002 race until the final weeks, when – in a pattern that would later become so familiar – he turned negative, and attacked his opponent with a blitzkrieg of hostile TV commercials. His big financial advantage proved crucial. How many of the dollars that paid for those commercials were Mormon dollars?

A look on the Federal Election Commission website tells a similar story since. Through March 31, 2012, Romney had raised millions from the Mormon states: $3.5 million in campaign contributions from Utah, $1.7 million from Arizona, $1.3 million from Colorado, $532,000 from Nevada, and $732,000 from Idaho. He raised more money from Utah than he did from Illinois, a state with nearly five times the population. In his 2008 campaign Romney raised more money in Utah, $5.5 million, than he did from any state other than California. Overall, from the main Mormon states – including Nevada, Colorado, Arizona and Idaho –

he raised nearly $10 million.

Those are the donations only to the official campaign. Restore Our Future, the "independent" Super PAC that whacked Romney's opponents in the primaries, received millions from wealthy individuals within the Latter-day Saints network, including $2 million just from the Marriott family.

The Mormon network gives Romney some big advantages. Yes, people are free to give contributions, and candidates are free to take them. But what is at question here is whether this is a two way street. If Mormon, Inc., can supply a presidential candidate with a lot of his money, network, and ideology, how can it not be acceptable to ask about it? Why should the Mormon church be shielded from the interest of the voters, when the voters are not shielded from the interest of the Mormon church?

Romney gets a lot of help from the LDS organization, politically as well as theologically. Ronald Scott, a fellow Mormon from Boston, tells us that as far back as 1994 Romney consulted the leadership of the church in Salt Lake City on how to handle the abortion issue when running for the Senate. He also reveals that in the first half of 2005, as Romney was first contemplating a run for the White House, he spent a lot of time in Salt Lake City seeking the advice of the church hierarchy, including Gordon Hinckley. "Basically, he camped out" at church headquarters, Scott quotes a senior church official as saying. (Massachusetts citizens who were wondering where their elected chief executive had disappeared to now have an answer.) Apparently Romney spent so much time with Hinckley, Scott said, that the Prophet got fed up.

This is mighty peculiar behavior for a man who insists that his faith is off limits to the voters. It is hardly surprising if voters want to ask questions about it. But Romney's blurring of political and religious lines hardly ends there.

According to the Associated Press, Gary Bauer,

president of the conservative Christian group American Values, once described gay civil unions as "worse than terrorism." In 2006 he took part in a bullying attempt to force Ford Motor Co. to withdraw all its advertising from gay publications and to boycott them. Richard Land, a senior figure within the right-wing Southern Baptist Convention, is a fundamentalist who has insisted that a truly Christian wife must "submit herself graciously" to her husband. The late Jerry Falwell, founder of the "Moral Majority," on the day after 9/11 blamed the terrorist attack on "pagans, and the abortionists, and the feminists, and the gays and the lesbians...I point the finger in their face and say: you helped this happen."

In October, 2006, all three men were guests of Mitt Romney near Boston. He wanted their advice on his run for the White House. Romney was worried that his membership of the Mormon church might prevent him from working the levers of the evangelical groups, so he sought help from Bauer, Land, Falwell and others.

There is something breathlessly cynical about someone who demands that the voters keep their noses out of his religion, while simultaneously trying to use as many religions as he can to shoehorn himself into office over them. Romney's game plan was accidentally revealed when Kem Gardner gave his mea culpa interview about the MVP. "We know Mitt can't use the church," he told the Salt Lake City Tribune. "Nobody wants a Mormon presidential campaign. It would kill us with the evangelical groups."

Here is the complete reversal of John Kennedy's ethos. Here is a belief in an America where the separation of church and state, far from being absolute, is nonexistent.

The table was set for this back in 2004, when John Kerry was running for president and Romney was an eager campaigner for the Bush-Cheney campaign. Raymond Burke, the Catholic archbishop of St. Louis, was quoted in the Associated Press shortly before the election saying that his fellow Catholic, John Kerry, should be denied the sacrament of Communion. A Catholic bishop in West Virginia said that voting for a pro-choice candidate (such as Kerry) amounted to "formal cooperation in grave evil." The Republican National Committee admitted sending out flyers in West Virginia and Arkansas saying that Democrats wanted to "ban" the Bible. It also contacted Catholics and Baptists who supported President Bush and asked for copies of their church rosters for campaign purposes, a move so over the line that even Richard Land said he was "appalled."

For anyone who believed seriously in John Kennedy's principles from 1960, or who wished to fight for privacy of religion, this was a moment ripe for an intervention. It was the perfect opportunity for a big speech demanding a halt to the madness. Mitt Romney was already a prominent public figure with a national platform. He would have assured widespread attention.

However, if he found these developments offensive, he kept his opinions to himself. While major figures within the Republican party fed Jack Kennedy's 1960 speech into the metaphorical shredder, the campaign echoed with Mitt Romney's silence.

9

WHAT WOULD MITT DO?

One of the candidates for president says he believes in global warming and calls the potential threat from the melting ice caps "truly alarming."

He likes the idea of taxing gasoline to encourage energy conservation, and of giving people a federal rebate when they buy more efficient cars. He calls failing public schools "the foremost civil-rights issue of our generation." He wants better teachers, even if that means fewer of them, and he wants to pay the good ones more. He praises equal opportunity labor laws, saying they "increase the inclusiveness of our economy, drawing people into the workforce who might otherwise have stayed on the sidelines."

That candidate is Mitt Romney.

To anyone who has followed Romney the politician over the years, a journey to the inner sections of his recent book *No Apology* is a surprising one. This is a very different person than the one we have seen running for president. He quotes Dr. Atul Gawande at length about the problems with the healthcare system. He cites detailed studies by Bain & Co. and McKinsey & Co. on class sizes, and on greenhouse gas abatement. He offers an idea worthy of George Romney's son for a goofy, fuel-efficient vehicle that could cut down on congestion. He writes with real engagement and knowledge about how to make schools better and how to protect the environment.

You can find a lot of this very interesting stuff in the second half of the book – right after the claims that Barack Obama hearts Fidel Castro.

What would Mitt Romney do if he were president? What are his ideas? A presidential race is such a fast-moving phenomenon that things change all the time. Yet in *No Apology* Romney took some time to set down some of his thinking on the big issues facing America.

There are some good, sensible and pragmatic ideas in here. Like any good consultant, he is absolutely at his best when he has pored through the data and crunched some numbers.

He is serious about alternative energy policy. He says he believes in global warming, and that our reliance on imported oil is a national security risk. His preferred solution: Raise the tax on fuel, and offset it, dollar-for-dollar, by cutting the payroll or income tax. It's a smart idea. Making energy more expensive is surely the best way to build a green economy. The consumers and investors, rather than the government, will end up picking the best companies and the best technologies.

He wants to get tough with China. He believes the country is manipulating its currency, and dumping goods here cheaply to take jobs. It's long overdue for people in Washington to take this stand. Romney, remarkably, says he is willing to drag China to the World Trade Organization and slap her with tariffs. He also says we should take a bold stand to support Taiwan's independence.

What about the looming budget crisis for entitlements? On Social Security, the idea he seems to like best is that offered by his friend Bob Pozen, the head of a mutual fund company in Boston, which involves slowing the rate of growth of benefits for higher earners. He's open to raising the retirement age for most workers. On Medicare, the bigger challenge, Romney sensibly says he wants to tackle rising healthcare costs by reforming the incentives in the system. We should stop paying doctors for performing procedures and tests, he says, and instead pay them for keeping people healthy. We also should give consumers better incentives to drive down costs, which likely means raising the amount that they have to pay. On Medicaid, he wants to hand the budgets over to each state.

He is very engaged on the subject of education. He wants to raise the starting salaries for teachers, pay good teachers more, and fire the bad ones. Numerous studies, he says, have shown that student performance is not about class size, it's about the quality of the teacher. We'd be better off spending our dollars on fewer, better teachers, even at the cost of bigger class sizes. This is an important and counterintuitive insight. He offers data to back it up.

There is nothing wrong with these proposals. Many of them are very good. They are what you might expect from a presidential candidate who is a pragmatic businessman and a moderate conservative.

Recently Mitt Romney has also unveiled a series of tax proposals. He says he wants to make permanent the "Bush" era tax cuts and the more recent fix to the Alternative Minimum Tax, both of which are due to expire at the end of this year. He wants to cut tax rates another 20% "across the board," abolish estate taxes, and cut corporation taxes. He also wants to raise defense spending to at least 4% of gross domestic product or more.

What can we make of these proposals?

To give you an idea, let's just look at what those policies

would do to the federal budget five years out. According to the Congressional Budget Office, currently we're on track for a budget deficit of about $220 billion by 2017. Romney's tax and defense proposals would hike that to $1.3 trillion.

Extending the Bush (and AMT) tax cuts alone would add $500 billion of that, says the CBO. By my math, Romney's additional tax cuts would add maybe $450 billion more. His defense spending boost would cost an extra $120 billion.

How would Mitt Romney pay for these cuts? On his campaign website he says he would privatize Amtrak, cut subsidies for the arts, end Title X family planning, and lower foreign aid. Mitt Romney has been spending too long hanging out at Republican debates. These four cuts in total would yield savings, he admits, of just $3 billion. He also says he would cut the federal workforce ($4 billion), reduce federal use of unionized contractors ($11 billion) and cut federal employees' pay ($47 billion). Of the bigger ticket items, Romney says he would save $95 billion a year by repealing ObamaCare and $60 billion by "reducing waste and fraud." Out of a Medicaid budget of about $400 billion, he claims his plan to let the states run it would save "$100 billion," or one dollar in four. We'll see.

Even these cuts, adjusted for inflation, would only save a total of $400 billion. This would still leave a deficit north of $900 billion.

He can't touch spending on debt interest ($400 billion) and he won't cut defense ($800 billion). That leaves spending on Social Security and Medicare ($1.7 trillion) and everything else ($1.3 trillion). Finding $900 billion in cuts from that should be interesting.

Understand, by the way, that these numbers from the CBO already take into account the deep, automated spending cuts agreed last year as part of the debt ceiling deal. Romney's extra savings would be in addition to those.

Any MBA graduate who turned up at Bain & Co. or Bain Capital offering this kind of math wouldn't get called back. Any analyst at either firm who produced this kind of report would be typing his resume.

Mitt Romney is good at math. He knows how to crunch numbers. So what is the explanation?

The really, really cynical explanation for these proposals is that although they would bankrupt the government, they would make Mitt Romney, his family, and his wealthy friends even richer than they are now. They would do the same for the hedge fund and private equity people financing his "independent" Super PAC.

Under Romney's tax plan, they would all get a 15% tax rate on most investment income, and a maximum rate of 28% on the rest. If the Bush tax cuts were to expire, they'd be paying 20% and 40%.

For Mitt Romney, based on his 2010 tax return, this would be the difference between paying less than $3 million in federal taxes and about $6 million. His proposal would, quite literally, halve his likely annual taxes.

As for the so-called "death tax:" Currently Mitt Romney's heirs are on track to pay up to $88 million, or 35%, when they inherit his $250 million estate. If the tax were abolished they would pay a lot less. Most of it would only be taxed as capital gains at 15%. And they wouldn't have to pay that until they sold assets.

By my math, that would save the Romney family at least $50 million.

The less cynical view of Mitt Romney's tax proposals is that he knows full well they are complete nonsense and that he never meant them for a moment. They were just another gimmick on the campaign trail. He produced them shortly before Super Tuesday, when he was trying to drive the proverbial stake into Rick Santorum.

While this explanation is more charitable, it leads to an obvious problem. It's one that runs throughout any assessment of Mitt Romney's life, politics and career. Yes, he's an intelligent man. He can give serious thought to major issues, and take a sensible, pragmatic approach to a problem.

But if he doesn't mean what he says, how can we know what he means? Or, to put it another way: When someone doesn't tell us the truth, what are they really telling us?

ABOUT THE AUTHOR

Brett Arends was a columnist for the Boston Herald during the Romney years. These days he writes about finance, markets and investing for the Wall Street Journal and Smart Money. That includes covering the private equity and hedge fund worlds where Mitt Romney made, and keeps, his money. Arends is a former consultant at McKinsey & Co., the strategy consultants. He has received an award from the Society of American Business Editors and Writers for distinguished commentary, and was part of the Herald team that won two others. He was born in Poughkeepsie, New York, but he has never played there. He was educated at Cambridge and Oxford universities in England. If Mitt Romney is elected president he hopes to land a posting to the Cayman Islands, where he will cover the president's money.

Printed in Great Britain
by Amazon

77528511R10088